Addict in the Family

Addict
in the
Family

Support Through Loss, Hope, and Recovery

SECOND EDITION

Beverly Conyers

Hazelden Publishing

Hazelden Publishing
Center City, Minnesota 55012
hazelden.org/bookstore

Library of Congress Cataloging-in-Publication Data

Conyers, Beverly, author.
Addict in the family: support through loss, hope, and recovery / Beverly Conyers.
Second edition. | Center City, Minnesota: Hazelden Publishing, 2021. | Includes
    bibliographical references.
LCCN 2021028405 (print) | LCCN 2021028406 (ebook) | ISBN 9781616499556
    (paperback) | ISBN 9781616499563 (ebook)
LCSH: Alcoholics—Family relationships. | Drug addicts—Family relationships. |
    Alcoholics—Rehabilitation. | Drug addicts—Rehabilitation.
LCC HV5132 .C645 2021 (print) | LCC HV5132 (ebook) | DDC 362.292/3—dc23
LC record available at https://lccn.loc.gov/2021028405
LC ebook record available at https://lccn.loc.gov/2021028406

Editor's notes:
This publication is not intended as a substitute for the advice of health care
professionals.
    All the stories in this book are based on actual experiences and personal
interviews. Names and certain facts have been changed to protect the
anonymity of the people who so generously shared their stories for this book.
    Readers should be aware that websites listed in this work may have changed
or disappeared between when this work was written and when it is read.

26 25 24 23   3 4 5 6

Art director: Terri Kinne
Cover designer: Nick Caruso Design
Typesetter: Percolator Graphic Design
Developmental editor: Marc Olson
Editorial project manager: Jean Cook

This book is dedicated to the Tuesday night group with heartfelt appreciation—and to my daughter with love.

Contents

Six: The Process of Change   89
Making a significant personal change is hard for everyone, especially for people who are seeking recovery. Change often occurs in predictable stages and usually involves setbacks and relapses.

Seven: Promoting the Addict's Recovery   107
No one can force another person to change. But families can practice strategies that effectively promote and support their loved one's recovery.

Eight: Promoting the Family's Recovery   135
Families suffer deep distress when a loved one becomes addicted. To recover from the damaging impact of the disease, they can adopt self-care strategies that nurture their own well-being.

Nine: A Time to Heal   147
In its deepest sense, recovery is a lifelong process of personal growth. It involves healing the wounds of the past to achieve greater wisdom and serenity.

Preface

It has been twenty years since I learned that my youngest daughter was addicted to heroin. At that terrifying moment of discovery, I could not possibly have anticipated the many difficult years that lay ahead. In my naivety, I imagined that, having uncovered her secret, I could soon find a way to make things right. After all, I had always been a problem solver. This situation, while scarier than most I'd encountered, would surely turn out to be just another bump in the road.

How wrong I was! Addiction would come to dominate her life and mine far into the future. I became more familiar than I ever wanted to be with things like detox, treatment, recovery, relapse, and the criminal justice system. I lived with deep anxiety and burgeoning hope and devastating disappointment. I learned about boundaries and detachment and letting go, about frustration and expectations and humility and forgiveness. And through it all, I learned about the boundless human capacity for starting over. And then starting over again.

I wrote *Addict in the Family* in my early years as the mother of an addicted child. My goals were to find answers to my many questions, to figure out how to help my daughter, and to help other parents who were struggling with a child's addiction. Over the years, much has changed. As a nation, we have experienced an explosion of opioid addiction. Science has delved deeper into the physiology of addiction. New approaches to treatment have emerged. Society is slowly coming to accept that addiction is a disease and not a moral failing. And my own understanding of addiction has been deepened by experience and by input from others.

As a result, the time seems right to offer a new, updated version of *Addict in the Family*—one that reflects the latest thinking on addiction and that builds on the experience, strength, and hope shared by many wonderful people I have met over the years. My dearest hope is that, for anyone who is coping with a loved one's addiction, this new edition will be a meaningful source of information, insight, comfort, and support.

Introduction

It is a Thursday night in late November. The sky is blanketed with low, thick clouds, the air heavy with impending rain. Bare branches of old trees carve faint silhouettes in a world of black and gray, relieved only by a single light above a narrow door and a horizontal row of five small square windows close to the ground and lit from within.

Inside the church basement, thirteen people sit around two rectangular folding tables pushed together to form a square. On the tables are books and pamphlets, a few bottles of water, and a box of tissues. The room is brightly lit by suspended fluorescent tubes, revealing pale yellow concrete walls, a green-and-white tile floor, and thin white curtains on the windows. The lights emit a faint whine, punctuated by the chirps and occasional clangs of three old radiators. No one pays any attention to the noises. All eyes are on Dot, a woman in her sixties with soft peach-tinted hair, a tired face made up in muted shades of pink, and sad blue eyes. She is, in her way, an attractive woman, with a large, soft body and a kindly face—the kind of face you associate with grandmothers who have spent their lives looking after their families and putting others first.

Tonight, Dot clutches a tissue in her hands. She announces to her support group, "He almost drowned in beef stew." Her voice holds amazement, as well as grief. "Honest to God. I was in the front room watching television with my husband. And something in the back of my mind says, 'David's been awful quiet,' so I went out to the kitchen, and there he was with his face in a bowl of stew. He didn't seem to be breathing. So I lifted up his head, and there was gravy and little bits of meat all over his face. 'You gotta stop this,' I said to him." She twists the tissue in her hands. "Honest to God. If I hadn't checked up on him, he would have drowned."

1

She is speaking of her thirty-six-year-old son, the baby of the family, the one who, as a little boy, had been the clown who made everyone laugh. A person couldn't be around David for five minutes without smiling at some silly thing he said or did—like the time during the third-grade Christmas pageant when he stood on stage with a dozen or so other children and sang both verses of "Silent Night" with his eyes crossed. She had wanted to kill him but ended up giggling instead.

Even now he can make her laugh, though tears are never far behind. David has been a heroin addict for eleven years and on methadone for the past three. She knows he still shoots up on occasion, but his latest thing is pills. He's been prescribed painkillers for a knee injury he got from falling down a flight of stairs. The pills are morphine-based. David has gone through a month's prescription in four days.

"I locked them up in my safe, but somehow he got into them," she tells her group. "A drug addict can get anything if he makes up his mind to do it, you know."

A few heads nod in understanding.

"The thing is, I didn't say anything to my husband. I didn't want to get him going, because he would've been off the wall. I just told David to go wash his face and put on a clean shirt." She shakes her head. "I'm learning."

There's an extended silence. No one rushes to fill it. It's as if the group has all the time in the world to think things over and wait for Dot to conclude her tale. One woman surreptitiously wipes her eyes, while a man gazes grimly at a distant wall. The sound of breathing blends with the faint whine of the lights. After two or three minutes, Dot says, "I thought it would be different when he came home this time. You know?"

She laughs, but there is no humor in the sound.

A few minutes later, a man is talking. He is a big man, broad shouldered and physically powerful. He wears metal-framed glasses with thick lenses that magnify his eyes, giving him an oddly vulnerable look. He owns his own business and is thinking about retiring in a few years. What is foremost in his mind tonight is his daughter Lila. She is twenty-two and has already caused him more heartache than his other three kids combined. After almost dying of anorexia in high school, she discovered pot in college and quickly moved on to crack cocaine and heroin. She dropped out of school in her sophomore year and moved with her boyfriend a couple of states away.

"She was home last week for Thanksgiving," he says, pushing his glasses up the bridge of his nose. "She looked pretty good. Thin but not skinny, thank God. I wouldn't want to go through that again." He squints, searching for words. "My wife said she was high, but I couldn't tell. She wasn't falling into her plate, anyway."

There are a few chuckles.

"I hated to see her go back, but I know she has to live her own life. I can't live it for her." Some nod in agreement.

"Anyway, my wife was changing the sheets after Lila left, and she found some clean needles under the mattress. I wanted to throw them in the garbage, but my wife said no. She said the next time Lila comes home we want her to have clean needles, don't we?"

A few people squirm, as if their chairs have become uncomfortable. "I'm still thinking about that one," he says. "I mean, I guess so. But I don't know."

The hands on the big round wall clock move on. "I could kill my sister for what she's doing to my parents!" exclaims a petite young woman. "I told him I'm not bailing him out this time," asserts a grim-looking man. "I went through it with my daughter, and now it's starting all over again with my grandson," says a slender woman with stylish white hair. Her voice is angry, but before she finishes speaking, her anger dissolves into tears.

One by one the members of the group speak. They talk of children and spouses, parents and partners, brothers and sisters. They share tales of deception, theft, jail, homelessness, institutions, sickness, and poverty—bleak narratives that document the destructive course of addiction. At the heart of every story lies the pain of having an addict in the family.

Few experiences in life quite match the feelings of horror, fear, helplessness, and grief that families experience when someone they love becomes addicted to alcohol or other drugs. They watch in dismay as the addict becomes alienated from the family and undergoes profound physical and emotional changes. Activities that once brought the addict pleasure are abandoned, old friends are pushed away, and the addict withdraws into a world that is increasingly inaccessible to anyone who tries to help.

Families ask themselves if their loved one is gone forever, replaced by an untrustworthy, soulless being like the empty-eyed creatures in *Invasion of the Body Snatchers*. More urgently, they ask themselves what they can do to effect a "cure" and get their loved one back to normal. They hope for a quick fix. Maybe detox and a good treatment facility will be all it takes. All too often, they end up joining the addict on the merry-go-round of denial, anger, confusion, and blame.

It's a depressing business, one that's experienced annually by millions of American families. The 2018 National Survey on Drug Use and Health found that "In 2018, approximately 20.3 million people aged 12 or older had a substance use disorder (SUD) related to their use of alcohol or illicit drugs in the past year, including 14.8 million people who had an alcohol use disorder and 8.1 million people who had an illicit drug use disorder."

Chances are someone in your family is among them. If that is the case, you have my sympathy. I have been in your shoes. The heroin addiction of my own daughter motivated me to write this book. After the initial shock of learning about her addiction, I began to look for answers to overwhelming questions: Had I caused her addiction? How could I have been so blind that I didn't see it sooner? What was it doing to her health, her happiness, her future? Was there any hope for her recovery? How could I help her get well? Was it possible to find any peace of mind and have a life of my own?

I found that while there were many books that dealt with various aspects of addiction and recovery, none seemed to fill my need for reliable information and helpful advice from people who had endured a similar crisis. I decided to expand my research to include alcohol and drug counselors, other families of addicts, and addicts themselves—both active users and those in recovery. This book is the compilation of what I have learned.

It does not promise simple solutions or definitive answers to all of your questions. That would be an impossible promise to keep. What it does offer is education and support in the form of practical information, advice from others who have been there, and the healing power of shared experiences. The real-life stories that people have shared in this book are intended to do much more than illustrate a point. They are intended to reduce the feelings of isolation often experienced by families who are coping with addiction and to be a source of comfort, insight, understanding, and hope.

ONE

A Family Disease

*"A major characteristic of genuine love is that
the distinction between oneself and the other
is always maintained and preserved."*
—M. SCOTT PECK

WHEN SHELLY BEGAN to talk about her daughter, she seemed to visibly shrink. Her shoulders slumped, her head drooped, and even the muscles of her pretty face went slack. She suddenly looked ten years older than the chic, petite blonde who had walked through the door only moments before.

"I know this is hard for you," I apologized.

She waved her hand and paused to gather her thoughts.

We were seated at a corner table set apart from the others in the bookstore café. Around us people chatted, laughed, or looked through the books and magazines set out for customers' enjoyment. There was a pleasant smell of coffee and baked goods.

The café was one of my favorite places, full of warmth and life. But in our little corner, the air was weighted with sadness. "If someone had told me two years ago that I'd be having this conversation, I'd have said they were out of their mind," she said with an attempted laugh. "Colleen was always the most responsible, considerate, and respectable girl you could ever meet. I don't think she ever even got a parking ticket."

I shook my head in sympathy.

"She had a perfect life. Everything she ever wanted. Her husband adored her. They had that sweet house and those beautiful babies." Her voice caught a little, and she swallowed some water before almost hissing out her next words: "And then she met that bum!"

"That bum" was a twenty-nine-year-old drug dealer named Marlon. How he and Colleen had met isn't clear, but soon after, her life took a 180-degree turn for the worse. She experimented with cocaine and in seemingly no time at all was hooked on crack. At first her husband had no explanation for Colleen's wild mood swings, evasiveness, irritability, and occasional incoherence. He urged her to see a doctor, but on the day of her appointment, he came home to find a note taped to the fridge: *Jeff, I'm sick of living for everyone else. I'm going to start living for myself.*

"She dropped the kids off at my house that day," Shelly remembered. "I thought she looked tired. And thin. Awfully thin. But I had no idea anything was going on. Jeff didn't say anything until later."

Colleen moved in with her dealer and quit her job as an insurance claims adjuster, a position she had held for more than four years. At first she visited Jeff and the children three or four times a week, but the visits tapered off to no more than once or twice a month.

Shelly speculated, "I think Jeff was relieved, in a way, because her behavior was so unpredictable that she upset the children. I think she scared them." Shelly's eyes filled with tears. "Can you imagine? My grandchildren being scared of their own mother."

After nearly a year of begging Colleen to get help, Jeff filed for divorce and was awarded full custody of their children. Although the divorce was not final when Shelly and I talked, she was certain that reconciliation would be impossible. "I think he hates her for what she's done to the kids," she said. "And all the rest of it. The lies, the stealing. He won't let her in the house anymore. Not since she walked out with all the electronics. We know where they ended up. At some pawnshop and up her nose."

Shelly's voice was harsh, but behind the anger was, I suspected, boundless grief. Her next words confirmed my thoughts. "Where will it end?" she whispered. "I think about it every waking moment of my life. No matter where I am or what I do, she's right there with me, filling up my head. Last month, my husband and I went away for a weekend just to clear our heads. We shouldn't have bothered. I was like a zombie. I was sick with fear the whole time. I can't stop worrying about what's going to happen to my daughter. I know she's done horrible, despicable things. But it's the drugs making her do it. It really is. Underneath it all, she's still a good person."

She wiped her eyes with a napkin. "I'm so afraid. She's my baby, and I'm so scared she's not going to make it." Her worry is not unwarranted.

A Deadly Toll

Drug overdose deaths in the United States have more than tripled in the past two decades, surpassing car accidents and falls as the leading cause of accidental death. The Centers for Disease Control and Prevention reported that from October 2019 through September 2020 there were an estimated 87,000 deaths from drug overdoses in the United States, an increase of 29 percent compared with the previous twelve months. Overdoses involving synthetic opioids such as fentanyl, fentanyl analogs, and tramadol jumped 10 percent from 2017 to 2018, while deaths linked to cocaine and psychostimulants such as methamphetamine more than tripled.

What's more, nonfatal drug-related poisonings in 2016 resulted in nearly 578,000 emergency room visits and an estimated 326,200 hospitalizations, according to the Centers for Disease Control and Prevention. And intentional overdose was the third leading method used in the suicides of more than 48,000 Americans in 2018. Alcohol addiction is equally devastating. The National Institute on Alcohol Abuse and Alcoholism reported that "The number of death certificates mentioning alcohol more than doubled from 35,914 in 1999 to 72,558 in 2017, the year in which alcohol played a role in 2.6% of all deaths in the United States." Nearly half of those deaths resulted from liver disease or overdoses on alcohol alone or with other drugs.

Beyond the statistics, addiction to alcohol or other drugs can tear families apart and plunge addicts into lives of poverty, homelessness, crime, and incarceration: an estimated 65 percent of the nation's approximately 1.43 million incarcerated people have a substance use disorder, and another 20 percent were under the influence of alcohol or other drugs at the time of their crime. Addiction stunts emotional and spiritual growth and ravages mental and physical health. Indeed, the consequences of the disease of addiction—which the National Institute on Drug Abuse defines as a "chronic, relapsing brain disease"—are as potentially devastating as those of most other major illnesses.

But the impact of addiction does not end there. For almost every addict who is mired in this terrible disease, others—a mother or father, a sister or brother, a partner or grandparent— are suffering too. Families are the hidden victims of addiction, enduring enormous levels of stress and pain. They suffer sleepless nights, deep anxiety, and physical exhaustion brought on by worry and desperation. They're haunted by a relentless drumbeat of "What if" and "If only," and their hearts are heavy with bottled-up anger, deep regret, or boundless sorrow.

Despite their suffering, families of addicts seldom receive the kind of support commonly extended to families of, say, cancer patients or stroke victims. Instead, they conceal their pain in the face of the all-too-common beliefs that addicts have only themselves to blame for their troubles, that addicts could cure themselves if they really wanted to, and that addicts' families probably did something "wrong" to cause the problem in the first place. Many families of addicts share these views, which only adds to their unhappiness.

"I could never tell anyone at work what's going on with Colleen," Shelly admitted. "They'd all look down on me. It's too horrible, too shameful."

Todd, a successful small-business owner, described his own feelings of guilt and shame about his twenty-eight-year-old son's alcoholism. "Watching my son throw his life away has been the most difficult experience of my life," he said. "The worst part is that I feel at fault. If I'd done things differently, he might not be where he is today, which is basically nowhere."

Searching for the root cause of the problem, Todd explained how he had worked long hours while his son was growing up. "I was gone three, four days every week. Maybe he thought I didn't love him. I don't know. Maybe he needed more discipline. Whatever it was, Mike went wild at an early age. By the time he was fourteen, he was emptying out the liquor cabinet and filling the bottles with water. I wanted to take a strap to him. That's what my father would've done. But his mother wouldn't hear of it and thought he needed counseling. Counseling! Forty thousand dollars of counseling! Mike's all grown up now except he's still like a little kid. I can't tell you the number of cars he has smashed up. And the jobs. Can't hold a job for more than a week. Of course he still lives with us. I don't see how he'll ever make it on his own."

Todd scratched his head, causing the silver-brown hair to stand on end. He took a long time getting to his next point, which for him seemed to be the most difficult. "I listen to our friends talk about what their kids are doing: graduating from college, starting careers, getting married, and settling down. Normal stuff, you know? I just change the subject. What did they know that I didn't? Where did I go wrong?"

Todd was voicing painful questions that haunt almost everyone who has ever loved an addict: "What could I have done to prevent this from happening?" and "What can I do to fix it?" He had not yet discovered the simple truth about addiction that is so hard for families to accept: You didn't cause it, you can't control it, and you can't cure it.

The Elusive Cure

It's normal to want to help those we love, especially when they are faced with a crippling condition such as addiction. However, the burden of guilt, the sense that we have somehow "caused" the addiction, can intensify our resolve to "cure" the addict, spurring us on to sometimes unhealthy and even counterproductive levels of involvement in our loved one's life. Parents, especially, look back on all the regrettable but inevitable mistakes of parenthood and feel a heavy sense of responsibility.

Even if we recognize that we didn't cause the addiction, most of us feel a desire, even an obligation, to do everything possible to rescue our loved one, spending enormous amounts of time, energy, and money in a desperate attempt to find a cure. But more often than not, the harder we try, the more our loved one resists our efforts.

This tug-of-war can last for years, with continued addiction and emotional exhaustion the inevitable results.

Missy, a divorced mother of two teenage girls, was engaged to a landscaper's assistant who played guitar in a local band most Friday and Saturday nights. She had met him at a club and was immediately attracted to his blond good looks. Early in the relationship, he had admitted to an on-again, off-again drug problem. After living with him for three months, she realized that the problem was mostly on and that the drug was heroin.

"I felt physically sick when I found out," she told me. "I mean, you hear all these stories about junkies, about how they'd kill their own mother for a fix, and here I'd brought this man into my house and made him a part of my family. At first I wanted to break it off, to end it right there. But I realized he was the same person I'd fallen in love with, except he had this big problem. I thought that maybe I could help him, that with my love and support he could get better."

Missy tried to take charge of her fiancé's behavior. She got him to check in to a rehab hospital for thirty days, and when he came home, she began to monitor his actions. She was afraid to let him out of her sight. When he did go out, she wanted to know where he was going, whom he was with, and when he'd be home. While he was gone, she went through his personal belongings, checking for hidden drugs. After only a week, she found a syringe. When she confronted him, he became angry. He said that the syringe had been there a long time and she had no right to go through his things. Worse, he said her hounding was making him crave drugs.

Missy tried to back off, but her suspicions ate away at her. Before long, she found herself following him around. Once, when he was parked in front of an apartment house where she suspected he bought drugs, she blocked his car with her own and waited for him to come out. He was furious when he saw her outside. They had a loud and prolonged argument in the street. "I must have looked like a crazy person," she said, blushing at the memory. "In a way, I was. I was out of my mind. I thought that if I screamed, nagged, or threatened him enough, he'd get clean. It didn't work."

In a way, Missy was fortunate. She eventually grew tired of her fiancé's increasingly irresponsible behavior and broke off the relationship. It is usually much harder for parents and other close family members to shut the addict out of their lives. Instead, when confronted with addiction, families are often drawn into painful, lengthy, and costly attempts to help their loved one recover.

"We could have bought New York with the money we spent on our daughter," declared Elaine, a schoolteacher whose husband owned a thriving real estate business. I met with her in her home, where a collage of photographs of her daughter at various ages hung on a wall in the living room. She was a pretty girl with a wide smile.

"She started with pot and alcohol when she was just a kid," Elaine explained. "When we found out, we got her into a rehab program out of state. She was there for six months, and when she came home, we thought we had the problem licked. She seemed so much better. Then she moved on to cocaine, so we sent her to a different place—someplace even more expensive. We figured the first program wasn't right for her. We just needed to find the right fit."

Elaine didn't realize it, but she and her husband had taken supporting roles in a painful drama that would drag on for the next eight years. Unlike a real dramatic play, however, each new act was a repetition of the first: their daughter would check into rehab, she'd be clean for a while, and then she would relapse and end up in rehab again.

"It was so discouraging," Elaine sighed. "And so predictable. She'd come home clean and full of enthusiasm about how she was going to turn her life around. A couple of times she was clean for more than a year. But then she'd start slipping, and before you knew it, she'd go right back to the drugs. We were out of our minds with worry."

In addition to paying for rehab, Elaine and her husband tried using rewards and bribery to help their daughter. "We'd say things like, 'Stay clean and we'll give you a car, or we'll pay your rent, or we'll send you on a vacation to someplace beautiful like the Bahamas.' I even made this reward chart, like she was in kindergarten or something. For every week she was clean, I'd treat her to a day spa, a new haircut, or new clothes or jewelry."

Elaine laughed ruefully. "It didn't work. Eventually I'd notice she wasn't wearing a necklace she especially liked, or that I hadn't seen a certain ring in a while. Things were falling apart again. She was hitting the pawnshops."

Other families engage in equally earnest but futile attempts to solve their loved one's addiction problems. They make counseling appointments, try to find their loved one a job, take charge of his or her personal hygiene, drive the addict to Twelve Step meetings, throw out alcohol or other drugs, supervise their loved one's diet, and try to prevent him or her from hanging out with the "wrong" people. They watch for every mood change with an eagle eye and obsessively monitor sleep patterns, appetite, pupil size, skin tone, and daily behavior. They nag, scold, threaten, and beg their loved one to get help and get clean.

For all their tears and heartache and desperately good intentions, most families are defeated in the end. Addicts persist in their self-destructive, addictive behavior until something *within themselves*—something quite apart from anyone else's efforts—changes so radically that the desire for the high is dulled and ultimately deadened by the desire for a better life.

The truth most families eventually discover is that no one can cure another person's addiction. Only addicts can do that for themselves.

Does this mean that families have no role to play in the miraculous process of recovery? On the contrary. Families can have a powerful impact on their loved one's struggle for recovery. Research shows that addicts who feel connected to a family that supports their recovery (even if that family is just one person) are more likely to stay clean than those who believe that no one cares.

However, there is a catch. The families themselves must be healthy if they hope to have a positive influence on their loved ones. Although this may seem self-evident, it is easy for families to lose sight of this truth as the disease of addiction threatens their own emotional health. Family members can lose their ability to think clearly and behave rationally when they get entangled in the world of addiction.

The process of addiction creates an alternate reality in the addict's mind. Thinking becomes distorted and values get twisted as the search for the next high takes precedence over every other consideration. Families, in their interactions with their loved one, get caught up in the insanity of the disease. Lines between reality and fantasy blur as families, in their desperate attempts to control and cure the addiction, begin to think and behave in ways that, upon reflection, make no sense. The more enmeshed family members become in their loved one's life, the more twisted their thinking is likely to become. As a result, their efforts to help grow increasingly futile, and their own well-being is compromised. A codependent relationship develops, harming both the addict and the family.

To prevent this unhealthy relationship from occurring, or to extricate themselves from such a relationship, families must arm themselves with as much knowledge about addiction as possible. They must understand what they can do to support the recovery process and learn successful strategies for coping with addictive behaviors. They must recognize common mistakes that may actually prolong addiction and avoid getting trapped in unhealthy patterns. Perhaps most important, they must reaffirm the value of their own lives and focus on their own peace of mind—regardless of what their addicted loved one does.

One of the most startling statements I heard in the early days of dealing with my daughter's addiction came from a recovering addict who told me, "Even if your daughter is living on the streets, you can still have happy days." It seemed unbelievable to me at that moment, yet after many months I came to see the wisdom of that remark. No matter how desperately I wanted to help my daughter, her life was separate from my own.

None of this is easy. Addicts' families walk an unhappy path that is strewn with many pitfalls and false starts. Mistakes are inevitable. Pain is inevitable. But these things can be accompanied by growth and wisdom and serenity when families approach addiction with an open mind, a willingness to learn, and the acceptance that recovery, like addiction itself, is a long and complex process. Families should never give up hope for recovery—for recovery can and does happen every day. Nor should they stop living their own lives while they wait for that miracle of recovery to occur. As a first step toward understanding the processes of addiction and recovery, the next chapter looks at some of the common—and confusing—behaviors that come with addiction.

TWO

The Stranger You Love

"Addicts don't have relationships. They take hostages."
—SAYING HEARD IN TWELVE STEP MEETINGS

ALL ADDICTS' STORIES are heartbreaking in their own unique ways. But if you hear enough of them, you begin to realize that they are also distressingly similar. They follow a predictable pattern of experimentation, habitual use, addiction, and eventual loss of everything most of us hold dear: family, friends, home, job, health, and personal values. Addicts become estranged from the nonaddicted world and seem not to mind when they are reduced to circumstances that would be intolerable to almost anyone who is thinking clearly. My own daughter was a prime example.

A heroin addict at age twenty-three, my daughter and her boyfriend, a fellow addict, were evicted from their apartment for not paying their rent. In the four months they had lived there, their apartment had become almost uninhabitable. The filthy bathroom contained a phone book that they used for toilet paper. The living room was a chaotic jumble of dirty dishes and soiled clothing and bedding. The bedroom floor was covered with animal feces from their cats and ferret.

They eventually moved in with friends for a short time and then to the back of their car, a small station wagon. By that time, they had lost or sold most of their possessions. Only a few items of clothing and some bedding remained. My daughter always wore the same long-sleeved shirt stained with sweat; the cuffs and sleeves were speckled with dots and streaks of blood. Her shoes smelled like rotten meat.

Yet when I confronted her about her situation, she insisted that nothing was wrong. "A lot of people live in their cars, Mom," she said, as if it were the most normal thing in the world. "We're going to get a new apartment next week. This is not a big deal." She denied the addiction outright.

As sickened as I was by her situation, I did not fully realize that I was dealing with someone who inhabited a mental world that was different from my own. Only later did I begin to see that we shared no common ground, that it was impossible for us to communicate because she had lost touch with everyday reality, and that my daughter had, in fact, become a stranger.

Most families of addicts experience similar feelings about their loved one. They say such things as "I don't even know who he is anymore" and "I look into her eyes and it's like there's no one there." One mother of an addict said to me with tears in her eyes, "What a terrible disease this is. It takes away our kids."

People sometimes claim that addicts have "lost their souls." What they mean is that people struggling with addiction no longer seem to care about anything but their drug of choice, that they have become untrustworthy, and that their value system seems bizarre or nonexistent.

Families experience a tremendous sense of loss as they see their loved one, who once possessed certain defining characteristics such as a good sense of humor or a strong work ethic or an affectionate nature, lose these positive traits. Indeed, individuality deteriorates as the addict takes on behaviors that are typical of other addicts, behaviors that are aimed at achieving one end: safeguarding their access to alcohol or other drugs.

Recognizable addictive behaviors, present to a greater or lesser degree in most addicted people, emerge as addiction takes hold. They are the result of a subconscious process in which new thought patterns are adopted to facilitate addiction. Addicts do not consciously decide to change their behavior. Rather, the process of change occurs at a deeper level, a result of the marvelous human capacity to adapt to altered circumstances. Addicts, not realizing what is happening, begin to think and behave in ways that may have been foreign before the addiction took hold, but that now seem natural and even necessary. Their brains have been biologically and chemically altered.

Families generally sense the changes in their loved one but do not fully appreciate the depth of those changes. They may continue to treat the addict as they have in the past, only to find their interactions with the addict increasingly confusing. They cannot find any solid ground in the changed relationship as the addict begins to exhibit a disturbing repertoire of addictive behaviors.

Foremost among these addictive behaviors is denial.

Denial

It is not uncommon in our society to hear someone described as being "in denial." This condition is generally understood to mean that the person in question is unwilling or unable to face the truth about a particular circumstance. Who among us hasn't been in denial about something, whether it's our relationships, our diet, our spending habits, or some other troubling aspect of our lives? Many families of addicts, including myself, deny their loved one's addiction for a long time before circumstances force them to face it. Denial seems to be a natural human response to situations we are unready or unable to cope with.

When applied to addiction, however, denial is taken to the extreme. Denial permeates all of an addict's thinking, blotting out reality and replacing it with a twisted perception that *everything* is other than what it is. The denial is most obvious when addicts are challenged to evaluate their own situation. They immediately deny that they have a problem and insist that they can control or stop their use of alcohol or other drugs whenever they choose.

Denise, a secretary whose seventeen-year-old son was hooked on heroin, described talking to him about the problem: "At first he said I was crazy, that I was imagining things. He kept telling me to leave him alone. He was really angry. But a friend of his had told me he was addicted, so I kept after him. He finally admitted to snorting heroin 'a little bit' at parties and things like that. He acted like it was nothing. Then he started stealing money from my pocketbook. All that time, I was confused because I felt things were bad, but he kept assuring me he had things under control. Then he sold his guitar, and I knew I couldn't go along with his denial anymore. I forced him to see a counselor. I found out he was shooting up four times a day. Even then, he still insisted he could stop anytime he wanted."

Peggy, married to a police officer addicted to cocaine, faced a similar experience. "He was spending every cent he made on cocaine," she said. "He stopped paying the bills, stopped buying groceries, so I had to take on all the household expenses. I kept threatening to walk out on him, and he kept saying I was crazy. He didn't have a problem. He was just fine. You know something? I honestly think he believed it. I don't think he had a clue about what was happening to him."

The pattern of denial that Peggy and Denise confronted is typical of most addicts. Denial is the mental mechanism that enables addicts to give up more and more of the things that are truly valuable in life in favor of a fleeting sense of well-being. In other words, denial is the foundation of addiction, the fertile soil in which it grows and flourishes. Denial provides the comforting delusion that everything is all right, smoothing the way for addicts as they wind deeper into their downward spiral.

A truism about addicts is that they will always deny their addiction or, if forced to admit it, they will minimize its depth. They consistently say such things as "I can stop any time I want" and "I only use it occasionally" and "I don't need help—there's nothing wrong." Even when everyone around them knows that addiction is destroying their lives, addicts will deny that they have a problem.

The depth of their denial does not stop there. As addiction takes its inevitable toll, addicts will also deny the severity of the consequences. Even as their world crumbles around them, as everything of value is stripped away, they will claim that their losses are not of much consequence. Their entire belief system is altered by the power of denial.

Jerry and Teresa, who had recently celebrated their thirtieth wedding anniversary, described their horror as their only daughter endured one tragedy after another without apparent concern. Their daughter was a nurse, a young mother in a committed relationship with her child's father. She became addicted to prescription drugs and lost her job. Soon afterward, she was arrested for forging prescriptions, then for shoplifting, and finally for prostitution. Over the course of several years, she spent many months in jail and lost her car, her apartment, and most of her possessions. Her partner left her, and ultimately, she lost custody of her child.

"It wasn't until we were awarded custody of our grandchild that I finally realized just how sick her thinking had become," Teresa said. "As she was being led off to prison and we were raising her child, her only comment was 'Well, it's only for nine months. I don't see what you're making such a big deal about.' Nine months! Nine minutes would have been too long for me to endure a situation like that. But she didn't seem to get it."

The power and importance of denial cannot be overstated when it comes to understanding addiction. Even when addicts are facing life on the streets or incarceration, they will deny that addiction is the root cause of their troubles. Their perception becomes so distorted by denial that they may be truly unable to comprehend the disaster that has befallen them.

Dishonesty

Closely related to denial is dishonesty. Dishonesty encompasses the evasiveness and lies, big and small, that addicts employ in their attempts to control their world, as well as the criminal behavior they may engage in to sustain their habit. A small joke that hints at the denial and dishonesty at the heart of the addict's world goes like this: An alcoholic will steal your wallet and lie about it. A drug addict will steal your wallet, then help you look for it.

Families dealing with addicted loved ones are dealing with liars. This statement may sound harsh, but it is almost always true. Addicts become master liars very early on. They learn to lie to conceal their habit. They lie so they can feed their habit. They lie to maintain their self-delusion about their habit. And finally, they lie because lying itself has become a habit.

One of the most difficult and painful aspects of my relationship with my daughter was trying to discern when she was lying and when she was telling the truth. Many of her lies seemed senseless to me, intended merely to keep me off balance or at a distance. Often in those early, edgy months of her attempted recovery, there were moments in which I believed genuine honesty had been achieved, only to later discover that whatever she had been telling me was pure fabrication. There came a time when I simply stopped believing anything she said.

Many families have had similar experiences. "I was worried about Abby for years before I learned about her crack addiction," said her father, a long-haul truck driver. "I knew something wasn't right, and I kept telling myself it was depression or PMS or growing pains—anything but drugs. I remember asking one of her friends if my daughter had a drug problem. Word got back to Abby, and she was furious, like I was the worst dad in the world. How could I even think such a thing about her? I felt like a jerk. Another time, I noticed a radio, TV, and other things of hers were missing. She said a friend had borrowed them. I remember saying half-jokingly that I hoped she wasn't pawning them. She asked what did I think she was? What kind of person goes around pawning things? Of course, I later found out that was exactly what she was doing. Everything she'd told me was a lie. But she was so convincing."

One mother described coming home to find a note from her son, who had been in recovery for some time. It said that he was out to lunch with his sponsor, the sponsor's treat. The mother felt good until the sponsor called that same day, asking for her son. The sponsor knew nothing about a lunch date and had not seen her son in some time.

Another mother remembered her daughter's elaborate lie about someone she had met in a support group: "She told me she'd met a nice woman named Maria who had three children. She told me this whole story about Maria's life and the hard times she'd been through and how she lived with her mother and on and on. I eventually found out there was no Maria. My daughter had made the whole thing up."

Another woman summed up her exasperation with her husband's lies by saying, "If he told me the sun was shining and I could see it with my own eyes, I still wouldn't believe him."

Lying not only conceals or minimizes an addiction problem; it also allows addicts to pretend that life is the way they wish it could be. Perhaps creating a make-believe world helps them feel better in some small, untouched core of their being. They may also lie to gain approval or to tell their families what they think their families want to hear. Although so much about people's personalities is altered by addiction, the human need for approval is strong and may well be a motivator behind some of the lies. However, regardless of their motives, when addicts lie, they undermine the trust that forms the basis of any healthy relationship. They create a huge gulf between themselves and their families, who end up feeling hurt, confused, and vulnerable.

Another facet of dishonesty is criminal activity. While not all addicts turn to crime, most of them will cross the line into illegal activities (that is, in addition to obtaining and using controlled substances) at some point during the course of their addiction.

My daughter and her boyfriend, for example, knowingly wrote a number of bad checks before local merchants caught on to them.

A former neighbor's husband, who unbeknownst to her had progressed from weekend cocaine use to full-time heroin addiction, repeatedly pawned the family's televisions and stereo equipment and claimed they were stolen. "I always wondered why ours was the only house that kept getting broken into," she recalled.

A mother of a crack addict kept her jewelry in a safe in the trunk of her car. "It was the only way I could think of to keep my daughter from stealing it," she said.

A father learned that his cocaine-addicted son had cleaned out the family checking account. "He's not living with us anymore, but I still hide the credit cards and keep my checkbooks and financial papers at work now in case he stops by the house," he told me.

Stories of theft, from a ten-dollar bill that disappears from someone's wallet to jewelry and other valuables that wind up in pawnshops, are common in families of addicts.

Shoplifting—for things to use or to sell for cash—is also common among addicts. This activity often brings them to the attention of law enforcement. "My daughter was never arrested for drugs," one mother said, "but she went to jail three times for shoplifting." One addict described a profitable variation on common shoplifting: an item is stolen from a store and then returned for a cash refund. "Not all stores will do it," she said, "but if you find a store that does, it pays better than pawnshops."

Some addicts progress from theft to burglary and robbery in an ever more desperate attempt to sustain their addiction. And some turn to prostitution. This is an especially painful reality for most parents to acknowledge. The father of a young woman addicted to crack cocaine expressed the feelings of many parents when he said, "I felt dead inside when I found out. I was numb for weeks. I couldn't accept the thought of my little girl out there selling herself to strangers."

Because of the blurring effects of dishonesty and denial, addicts themselves are able to rationalize and minimize the corrupting influence of addiction. Often, they seem unaware that their values have deteriorated. Families observe the downward slide with a growing sense of helplessness, a condition that works to the addiction's advantage.

Manipulation

Manipulation is an indirect attempt to get others to fulfill our desires. It's a skill that most of us learn early on. For example, babies learn how to use tears or smiles to get their needs met, and toddlers and young children throw tantrums, pout, whine, beg, and wheedle to get their way. Adults, too, may try to manipulate others, sometimes without even realizing they are doing it. When we lie, withhold information, cajole, threaten, or otherwise do things intended to control someone's behavior, we're engaging in manipulation. While some forms of manipulation may be relatively harmless, highly manipulative adults are almost universally viewed with distaste, and their actions are often destructive.

Addicts are master manipulators. No matter how irrational and self-defeating their behavior may seem, addicts often get just what they want from those who care most deeply about them. Like other manipulative people, the tools they most often use are fear, guilt, and pity.

Fear

Families suffer a great deal of fear when a loved one succumbs to addiction. They fear public humiliation, the disgrace of having an addict in the family. They fear for the addict's future, for the loss of home, health, and income. If the addict is a parent, they fear for the well-being of the addict's children. And almost universally, they fear for the addict's life.

One father put it succinctly: "We're afraid our daughter is going to die."

Another parent said, "We were convinced they were going to find her body in a Dumpster someday."

A mother said of her son, "My biggest fear is that he'll end up living on the streets, that he'll become one of those bums you see lying in a doorway somewhere, that people will just step over him like he's a piece of trash."

A sister of an alcoholic told me, "I'm afraid he's going to kill somebody when he's out there driving around out of his mind. I don't think my parents could handle that."

It is all too easy for families to fear the worst when they are trying to cope with addiction. The bizarre world of addiction makes almost any terrible event seem possible and even likely. Families learn to fear the ringing of the telephone or an unexpected knock on the door. They become afraid when they haven't heard from the addict in a while and, if the addict has episodes of anger or violence, are even more afraid when the addict shows up at their door.

The fear that springs from the family's love and concern for the addict becomes one of the addict's favorite weapons in the game of manipulation. It is very hard to say no to somebody when you fear the consequence might be that person's death. It is hard to stand your ground when you fear that your loved one will end up behind bars or living on the streets.

Jerry and Teresa, whose daughter had become addicted to prescription drugs, described a scene in which they tried to force her to check into a residential treatment program. The daughter, who was living in their home at the time, insisted she wasn't ready. Teresa recalled: "Feelings escalated and she was crying, and finally she started throwing her clothes into a black garbage bag. She said she couldn't take the pressure of living with us and was going to go check into this shelter that had a terrible reputation for being full of drugs and violence. The thought of it terrified me. So when she said that's where she was going, my heart just broke. I couldn't stand the thought of my little girl in that place. I started crying, and the next thing I knew, I was begging her to stay. She didn't have to go into a program if she wasn't ready. I backed down completely."

Teresa said that, looking back on the incident, she can see that she was being manipulated. But all she felt at the time was fear for her daughter's safety. That's why she let her daughter stay home and continue to use drugs.

Guilt

Guilt is another favorite manipulative tool of addicts. Addicts commonly try to find someone to blame for their situation, and that someone is frequently a parent, spouse, or other family member.

Most parents, when looking back on how they raised their children, have at least some regrets. They may wish that they had been more or less strict, that they had expected more or less of their children, that they had spent more time with them, or that they had not been so overprotective. They may reflect on difficult events, such as a divorce or death in the family, and see these as turning points in their child's mental health. Some may bear heavy burdens of shame over past mistakes, such as an infidelity or the parent's own substance abuse. Whatever the parental failings may be, it is almost inevitable that the addict will recognize these vulnerable spots and take advantage of them. Here's an example of how it works.

Judy's first husband was an alcoholic who abused her and terrorized the children when he was drunk. Because they had been high school sweethearts and she loved him and kept hoping he'd change, she stuck by him for nearly ten years before getting a divorce. Twenty years later, her oldest son, then twenty-eight, had become a heroin addict. Judy was devastated and consumed with guilt. If only she'd left her husband sooner, if only her child hadn't witnessed the violence, if only he hadn't lived with so much chaos, he would never have turned to drugs. His addiction was her fault. This was what she told herself. It was also what her son told her.

Whenever Judy brought up the subject of his addiction, whenever she urged him to seek help or refused to "loan" him money, he countered with the bitter reminder that it was all her fault. Her guilt would resurface, and she would drop the subject or give him what he asked for.

In an effort to manipulate, addicts are apt to tell their parents such things as "You didn't love me enough" or "Nothing I ever did was good enough for you" or "You were never the father I needed you to be." One young woman angrily told her parents, "You never listened to what I wanted. You forced me to take dancing lessons even though I hated them." Another, the child of an alcoholic mother, told her older sister, "You abandoned me when you went to college. If you'd cared about me, you wouldn't have left me with Mom."

Between spouses, the guilt game may take a slightly different twist. Addicts may try to induce guilt by singling out personal "flaws" as well as past behaviors. They say such things as "I wouldn't have to drink so much if you could keep these kids under control" or "I wouldn't have to use drugs if you were more fun (or good-looking or sexy or interesting or rich)." This type of finger-pointing is pure manipulation, but spouses often feel a guilty sense of responsibility for addicts' problems.

Addicts typically have many complaints, including major and minor grievances from years past. Some of their accusations may, in fact, have truth in them. Families may well have caused their loved one pain. They may well have failed the person in some significant way. (After all, what human relationship is perfect?) But addicts bring up these problems not to clear the air or with the hope of healing old wounds. They bring them up solely to induce guilt, a tool with which they manipulate others in pursuit of their continued addiction.

Pity

Another common manipulative tool is pity. Addicts are, in general, pitiful people. Many of them struggle with depression, anxiety disorders, and other emotional problems. Many suffer from social alienation, shattered relationships, and loneliness. Most are burdened with overwhelming problems such as bad

credit, debt, and marginal employability. The difficulties resulting from addiction can be truly momentous, arousing a great
deal of concern and pity in those who love the addict.

Most addicts are not averse to using this pity to their own
advantage, as Doreen and Jake's story illustrates. Doreen, a
motherly woman in her late fifties, worked in a nursing home
as a nurse's aide. It was a physically grueling job, requiring her
to lift patients, make beds, change diapers, empty bedpans, and
provide general care for ten or more elderly patients every day.
Doreen suffered from chronic back pain and a bad knee, but
she worked all the overtime she could get in order to support
herself and Jake, her thirty-eight-year-old son.

Jake had been an alcoholic since his mid-teens. He had lived
independently in his early twenties, but after several failed relationships, he moved in with his mother. Once there, he seemed
to require more and more care. Doreen worried about his
health, so she cooked a nutritious meal for him every day. She
worried about his lack of grooming, so she did his laundry and
forced him to shower. She even cut his hair when he had no
money for the barber. She worried about his general aimless-
ness and lack of motivation, so she drove him to his counseling
appointments and to job interviews.

Sometimes Doreen felt resentful and threatened to throw
him out. Then he would say something such as "I don't blame
you, Ma. No one would want me," and pity would make her
relent. One day he took her car without permission (as he often
did) and got into a serious accident. One of his legs was permanently damaged. He took to lying in bed or on the couch
for hours on end, smoking cigarettes and watching television.
The only time he was motivated to move was when he ran out
of alcohol, at which point he would hobble to the corner store.

Doreen suggested that if he was healthy enough to get alcohol, he should be healthy enough to get a job and move out. But

he said, "You're so hard, Ma. I need something for the pain. Besides, where would I go? No one wants an old cripple like me." Again, pity made her back off, and her son got exactly what he wanted: a comfortable home in which to indulge his addiction.

Not all addicts are as overt in their bids for pity. Some—such as the heroin addict who has been evicted from his apartment and has no place to go or the crack addict whose skeletal appearance suggests imminent death—arouse pity merely by the circumstances of their lives. Families, taking pity, want to provide a home or buy groceries or otherwise take care of their pitiful loved ones. My own daughter, who often seemed depressed and listless, aroused so much pity in me that I bought her a car, thinking that would cheer her up. A month later, she and her boyfriend were living in the car, so I let her move into my house. There, I reasoned, she would be free to focus on her recovery.

Three cars and several thousand dollars later, I realized that buying cars for her was not the answer to her problems. Neither, perhaps, was letting her live with me. She continued to use heroin despite her promises not to, and whenever I approached the subject, she would react either with anger (which she soon discovered did not work to her advantage) or with tears (which often worked). She would say that she was trying, but that she was so lonely, that she had no friends, and that her life was pointless and empty. The topic of conversation would then shift from her addiction and what she was doing about it to her pervasive sadness. I believe that the sadness was genuine, but I eventually came to see that when my pity kicked in, she gained the upper hand in the conversation. The focus would shift from a topic that made her uncomfortable—namely, her addiction and what she was doing about it—to a more comfortable one of casting herself as a victim in a situation over which she had no control.

Because pity usually reinforces addicts' sense of helplessness, it can be very damaging in their search for recovery. But as a manipulative tool to enable them to continue using, it is very effective.

Symptomatic Behaviors

In my experience, denial, dishonesty, and manipulation are the behaviors most commonly used to facilitate addiction. They are the behaviors addicts call on time and again in the all-consuming effort to get drugs, use drugs, and conceal the addiction from others. These behaviors become like second nature, helping the addiction take root and blossom.

However, there are other confusing, even bizarre behaviors associated with addiction that result from the effects of the alcohol or other drugs themselves. They include withdrawal from family and friends, defensiveness, lack of responsibility, lack of personal hygiene, and irrational and inexplicable mood swings.

My daughter exhibited all of these behaviors over two terrible years before I finally acknowledged her addiction. I kept trying to convince myself that she was suffering from nothing more serious than mild depression. She was living with her boyfriend in an apartment about a fifteen-minute walk from my house, yet I rarely saw her. She avoided answering the phone or opening the door when I rang her bell. Once she was coming out of her building just as I was arriving, and she became hysterical. "Why can't you leave me alone? Why are you always bothering me?" she cried. I had never seen her so frantic and had no idea at the time that she was coming down from a cocaine high.

On another occasion, after her phone was disconnected and neither her friends nor I had heard from her in more than a week, I became so alarmed that I asked her landlord to let me into her apartment. I had been ringing her bell and knocking on her door off and on for most of the day with no response. As he inserted the key, he banged on the door, and I called out her name yet again. There was no response, so he pushed the door open. I was convinced that she had moved away or was dead. Instead, as the door opened, my daughter and her boyfriend jumped up from their futon, not more than three feet from the door, with a surprised exclamation of "What the fuck!" Anger and accusations followed. "You're psychotic, Mom!" she screamed. "Why can't you accept that I'm grown up? I don't have to be hanging out with my mother anymore."

The refusal to answer the door became a common thread throughout her addiction to cocaine and then to heroin, as did her reluctance to participate in family gatherings or join me in activities she had once enjoyed, such as going to the movies or going out to eat. She became increasingly isolated and treated every overture of kindness from her friends, her siblings, and me as an invasion of her privacy. Her rare interactions with the family usually resulted in scenes of rage or tears. Amazingly, through it all, I persisted in my own denial of her drug problems, although they were the obvious explanation for the terrible changes I was seeing in her.

Another mother told me of a similar experience with her son, a thirty-two-year-old licensed electrician. "He used to be so responsible," she said. "He made good money and had some close friends, and I thought he was set for life. Oh, I knew he smoked pot, but I didn't consider it a problem. He had a good head on his shoulders. Then everything fell apart. He stopped paying his rent. He wrecked his truck and lost his job. His phone and electricity were shut off, and he stopped coming around to visit. We all saw him less and less. Looking back, there were plenty of red flags, but I didn't see them.

"Finally, he admitted to his brother that he was hooked on heroin. When I learned the truth, I went over there and banged on his door for at least an hour. I was screaming his name at the top of my lungs. The neighbors must have thought I was a crazy woman. Finally, I said I was going to get the cops to break down the door because I really thought he must be dead in there. What else could I think? That's when he opened the door. He looked awful, thin and sickly. He let me in, but he turned his back to me. He kept saying he just wanted to be left alone. Why couldn't I just leave him alone? I started yelling at him. I couldn't help myself. I kept asking how he could be so stupid, things like that. I was out of my mind. After a while, I don't know how long, he just broke down and sobbed. He was like a little boy."

Her anger at her son's "stupidity" was mingled with disbelief. "It was like a nightmare," she recalled. How could drug addiction change her son from the clear-headed, hardworking young man she had always known into the irresponsible emotional wreck she saw before her? It seemed impossible that this weeping, fragile man was truly her son.

Yet the kind of transformation she witnessed in her son is one that is seen all too often by families who are struggling with addiction. Families try desperately to say the right word or do the right thing that will snap their loved one out of the insane behavior. They try reasoning, threatening, or using any tactic that may formerly have affected the addict's actions. But their efforts are usually futile—for the simple reason that the addict's brain has been dramatically altered by addiction.

Scientists have made great strides in understanding how addiction alters the brain. What has become increasingly clear is that giving up alcohol or other drugs is not a simple matter of choice or willpower. The addicted brain itself functions differently from a nonaddicted brain, and addiction affects every aspect of a person's mental, physical, and emotional existence.

This knowledge is terrifying for most families, driving home the point of just how appalling their loved one's condition is. But there is also strength in knowledge. No addiction is hopeless, and by understanding how addiction works, families can find effective strategies for coping with this life-altering disease.

THREE

The Beast Inside

"At first, addiction is maintained by pleasure,
but the intensity of this pleasure gradually
diminishes and the addiction is then maintained
by the avoidance of pain."
—FRANK TALLIS

JOHN, A RECOVERING CRACK ADDICT whose grown children were fighting their own battles with addiction, described how hard quitting for good had been for him thirteen years earlier: "Their mother had walked out on us, and I knew I was in danger of losing my kids if I didn't get clean. I was scared and motivated to stop using. I can't tell you how many times I'd get off work and tell myself, 'I'm not going to use. I'm not going to use.' But then I'd call my dealer and drive over to his house, still thinking, 'I'm not going to use. I'm not going to use.' I'd give him the money, cook up the dope, and put it in the pipe, all the time telling myself, 'I'm not going to use.' Then I'd light it up, smoke it, and say, 'Damn! I used again.'"

As John explained it, when he started getting serious about getting clean, he often felt like two people: the good father who wanted to do right by his kids and the addict who cared only about getting high. According to him, "It was almost as if there was this other person living inside me, this crazy person I couldn't control."

My daughter described a similar feeling one night, crying, "Sometimes I feel like there's a beast inside me."

Whether it's a beast inside or a monkey on the back, addiction has the power to wipe out reason, willpower, and good intentions. It creates a perverted reality within the mind, in which obsession with the addictive substance obliterates the capacity for rational decision-making. This condition is not a figment of the addicted person's imagination. Addiction works by actually altering normal brain function.

In its simplest terms, addiction can be viewed as a combination of two circumstances: physical dependence and obsessive thinking. Both cause the addict's life to revolve around getting, preparing, and using alcohol or other drugs.

No one sets out to become an addict. No one decides one day, "I guess I'll use this drug until I become addicted, and then I'll just go ahead and alienate everybody I know and lose everything of value." Instead, addiction begins deep within the brain with physical and chemical changes to the systems that process information. Of particular significance is the way that addiction changes the experience of pleasure.

We are all born with the capacity to feel pleasure. From a strictly biological perspective, pleasure is a survival mechanism. Food and sex can trigger intense feelings of pleasure, and both are fundamental to our survival as a species. Other pleasurable experiences, including satisfying relationships, personal accomplishments, and the appreciation of natural or artistic beauty, add meaning and purpose to life.

We can all name specific experiences that produce sensations of pleasure and describe what those sensations feel like. But scientists can go even further. They can identify the electrical and chemical activities that occur within the brain to generate those good sensations.

The Biology of Addiction

The brain's reward center—a circuit of electrical impulses and chemical messengers located in the two central gray areas of the brain—is responsible for our ability to experience pleasure. When we eat a good meal, have satisfying sex, connect with friends, or engage in other fulfilling activities, this area of the brain releases dopamine, endorphins, and other neurotransmitters—miniscule messenger chemicals that carry messages of pleasure, calm, relief, and euphoria. (The brain also has neurotransmitters that carry messages of pain, fear, anger, and so on.) The chemical messengers then connect with targeted receptors that fire off pleasurable sensations.

From an evolutionary viewpoint, this process in the brain promotes behaviors that support the survival of our species (eating, procreating, and social bonding) and eases physical suffering. When we talk of a "runner's high" or "endorphin rush," we are referring to the feeling of well-being and exhilaration that can follow an episode of pain, danger, or stress. Anorexia, for example, triggers the release of endorphins as the body attempts to ease the distress of starvation. And most of us who have experienced the ordeal of childbirth have also experienced the feeling of profound well-being that floods the body soon afterward.

Addictive substances work on the brain's reward center either by mimicking the brain's own pleasure messenger chemicals, or by overstimulating the reward center to release more of those chemicals.

Some drugs, such as marijuana, heroin, and narcotic painkillers, are similar in structure to dopamine and endorphins, the pleasure-producing neurotransmitters. When these drugs enter the brain, they connect with receptors in the reward center in the same way as their naturally occurring counterparts. This means that users experience calm, contentment, and euphoria simply by shipping the imitation pleasure messenger chemicals to the brain, without engaging in any of the rewarding activities that would ordinarily lead to such a flood of pleasure.

Other drugs, such as cocaine and methamphetamine, trick the brain's reward center by causing it to release abnormally large amounts of neurotransmitters—primarily dopamine—or by stopping the normal recycling process in which neurotrans-mitters are reabsorbed by the brain. As a result, the user's brain is awash in dopamine and other pleasure messenger chemicals, producing an exaggerated sense of well-being and feelings of energy, alertness, and confidence.

Alcohol also stimulates the release of neurotransmitters, including dopamine and gamma-aminobutyric acid (GABA), which reduces anxiety and causes drowsiness. In the early stages of intoxication, we may feel unusually happy, lively, or aggressive. But as the GABA takes effect, we are likely to want only to sleep.

Regardless of how mood-altering chemicals achieve their effects, the process of becoming addicted is the same for almost everyone. At first, we use because it makes us feel good—so good, in fact, that we want to do it over and over again. But the more chemicals we send to the brain, the more the brain tries to re-establish a balance. It does this by producing fewer plea-sure neurotransmitters of its own or by reducing the number of receptors available for the chemicals to connect with.

As a result, dopamine and other pleasure neurotransmitters have a weaker impact on the reward center, and this in turn diminishes the "high." Not only is the pleasure of using dimin-ished. The user's ability to enjoy *anything* is also diminished, because the brain's reward center is damaged. According to the National Institute on Drug Abuse (NIDA), "This decrease [in pleasure neurotransmitters] compels the addicted person to keep using drugs in an attempt to bring the dopamine function back to normal, except now larger amounts of the drug are required to achieve the same dopamine high—an effect known as tolerance."

As one addict explained tolerance, "I know it sounds weird, but when you're physically addicted, you need it so you won't get sick. You need it to feel normal. You don't get high. You feel relaxed, numb, kind of happy."

But the desire to feel "normal" is not what propels addiction along its disastrous course. Rather, addiction is fueled by the irresistible compulsion to experience again and again the rush of pleasure—the high. To achieve this, addicts must either be clean for a period to lower their tolerance level (some people go in and out of detox for this very reason) or continually increase their intake of alcohol or other drugs.

Compounding the problem, the damaging effects of addictive substances extend far beyond the brain's reward center. Research has shown that long-term abuse causes changes in other brain functions as well. According to NIDA, "Brain imaging studies of drug-addicted individuals show changes in areas of the brain that are critical to judgment, decision-making, learning and memory, and behavior control. Together, these changes can drive an abuser to seek out and take drugs compulsively despite adverse, even devastating consequences—that is the nature of addiction."

Brian, a thirty-one-year-old college student who was homeless for ten years, knows firsthand the dangerous downward spiral of addiction as well as the poor decision-making that comes with it. "My father and grandfather were both alcoholics, so I grew up knowing I should never drink," he said. "I figured pot was a safe alternative."

He started "partying" in his early teens, and before long he was skipping school to get high. "My mother and grandmother always told me I was going to be a doctor or a lawyer someday. School came easy for me, but when I got into higher math classes and things started getting harder, I'd go get high instead of doing the work," he recalled. He dropped out of school, got a GED, and started working as a cook. "I told myself everything was great. But inside, I blamed myself for losing my future."

By then he was experimenting with ecstasy and coke, but it was a serious car accident that introduced him to opioids. After a week in the hospital, doctors sent him home with a massive prescription for oxycodone. "They gave me pills I didn't even know existed, like a flashlight stick bottle full," he said. "So I went from partying and bad decisions to dependency."

Other drugs had never "done much" for him, but his first opioid high was a revelation. "When I got out of the hospital, I smoked some pot and took some pills, and I got this warm, fuzzy, neck-warming, cozy feeling. It just hit me, and I knew it wasn't the pot. And I thought, 'I want to feel like this the rest of my life.' I felt motivated, like Superman. Like, 'This is what I want. This is it.'"

Before long, he was "making bad decisions left and right, stealing percs from my girlfriend's mother, writing checks to myself from my boss's checkbook." He didn't know it then, but his steep slide into homelessness had just begun.

For Mark, a married father of two who often worked two jobs during many years of active alcoholism, the progression of the disease was more gradual, a "very slight" downhill slope. "When I got married, I was drinking two or three beers a day during the week and drinking all day and into the evening on weekends. Then I started going out for noon beers, especially on Fridays. Then it turned into Thursdays, Wednesdays, every day. I was drinking three-quarters of a case of beer a day, maybe more, and three or four shots of whiskey," he said.

"I wouldn't feel so good when I woke up, so one day I had a couple of shots or beers to straighten me out in the morning. It worked, so I did it again, and it turned into three or four or as many as I could get before I got into the shop." His family was putting pressure on him to cut down, but "at the end, the drinking was continual."

The need to use ever greater quantities of the substance that once brought so much pleasure is the direct result of changes to brain functioning. Not only do addicts find it increasingly difficult to experience the pleasurable effects they felt early in their substance use, but their brains also lose receptivity to the normal pleasures of food, beauty, companionship, and sex. Those ordinary pleasures fail to stimulate the brain, which has been altered by continual substance abuse. To the addicted brain, the chemical high becomes not only an intense source of pleasure, but also the *only* source of pleasure.

Jane, a mother of two whose heroin addiction led to the loss of her children, multiple prison sentences, and life on the streets, said that losing those things was not enough to make her stop using drugs, because none of them brought her the pleasure that drugs did. She said, "I loved shooting dope. It made me feel good. It was what I lived for."

Further deepening the process of addiction is the flip side of pleasure: pain. Sigmund Freud asserted that "our entire psychological activity is bent upon producing pleasure and avoiding pain." Certainly, addicts suffer both psychological and physical pain as a consequence of their addiction. When deprived of its customary drugs, the chemically addicted brain experiences an onslaught of stressful responses, such as fear, anxiety, panic, and severe depression. Withdrawal can also produce physiological symptoms that include persistent discomfort, intense pain throughout the body, digestive disorders, seizures, strokes, and even death. Addicts describe periods of drug deprivation with such phrases as "I was crawling out of my skin" or "I had the shakes so bad I couldn't walk."

The addicted brain, when in distress, craves the drug that has consistently provided relief from pain. In this way, positive reinforcement (pleasure) combines with negative reinforcement (relief from pain) to tighten the grip of addiction.

Of course, the human brain functions as much more than a vehicle to process pleasure and pain. It is, in fact, our primary survival tool. Our brain and its miraculous ability to reason, assess situations, solve problems, and predict consequences enabled us to become the dominant species on the planet. Without our incredible brains, we physically vulnerable humans may well have become just another failed evolutionary experiment.

Unfortunately, addiction short-circuits higher mental functions by concentrating the brain's energy on the obsessive pursuit of pleasure. In his book *The Selfish Brain,* former U.S. drug czar Robert L. DuPont, MD, says, "Addiction is a perversion of brain biology . . . because, unlike feeding, aggression, and sex, there is no biological purpose to the use of addicting drugs. Addiction is brain stimulation devoid of biological meaning."

The Psychology of Addiction

Anyone who has witnessed the downward spiral of an addict's life has been frustrated and bewildered by the addict's repetitious pattern of poor choices and disastrous consequences. As we have seen, biology is partly to blame because psychoactive substances dramatically alter brain functioning. Less understood is the psychological imperative behind addiction. Like certain forms of mental illness, addiction is a disease that consistently tells the victim there is nothing wrong. The addict's life may be falling to pieces, everything of value may be slipping away, but the addicted brain says such reassuring things as "You're okay" or "You can handle this" or "You don't have a problem—*they* do."

To make matters worse, these twisted perceptions are validated by substance-generated feelings of intense pleasure—a perverse fusion of false perceptions and biological reinforcement.

To begin to understand the psychological basis of addiction, we must first recognize that it is fundamentally obsessive-compulsive in nature. Obsessive-compulsive disorder is a mental illness that causes persistent unwelcome thoughts and images accompanied by the irresistible urge to perform repetitive actions or rituals. This serious condition can interfere with a person's ability to live a normal life, and many who suffer from it can recover only with the help of psychotherapy and sometimes medication.

For people with addictions, powerful obsessive-compulsive urges center on obtaining, preparing, and using alcohol or other drugs. Like others afflicted with this condition, addicts are unable to control their thoughts, and they feel compelled to use again and again, despite the severe consequences that result from their actions.

Lia, a twenty-two-year-old college student, described the urges she experienced as an active addict: "Drugs were the only thing I thought about from the moment I started to wake up to the time I went to sleep. I even dreamed about them. I couldn't escape thinking about drugs, and the thoughts were so huge there wasn't room for anything else."

A young mother recalled, "I used to think about drinking all the time. It was always in my head, you know, when I was going to buy it, where I was going to drink it, how I was going to hide it. And once I took a drink, I couldn't stop. I always had to have more until I passed out."

The urge to use takes on a psychological life of its own, making relapse a prevalent problem among the addicted population. Being clean, even for extended periods, and allowing the brain to return to normal biological functioning sometimes does little to prevent the obsessive thinking and compulsive urges that can lead recovering addicts to resume their use of alcohol or other drugs.

The obsessive-compulsive nature of addiction extends beyond the substance itself to encompass people, places, and paraphernalia—everything associated with the process of getting high. Crack addicts can experience pleasure just by looking at their blackened fingers. A heroin addict said, "I loved the low-down, dirty lifestyle that goes along with being a junkie." Another addict explained, "You sort of get addicted to the whole drug lifestyle, the process of getting drugs, how you get high, whom you get high with, what you do for money. It's so baffling, but it's more than the drugs. It's the whole process, preparing the needle, hearing the whoosh when it sucks up the drugs, cooking coke on the stove, shooting it into your arms, all of that."

Psychologically, these feelings can be explained by the phenomenon of association. Most of us are familiar with Ivan Pavlov's famous experiment in which he always rang a bell before feeding his dogs. In time, they came to associate the sound of the bell with the pleasure of eating, and the bell alone would cause them to salivate. Similarly, addicts associate certain places and experiences with pleasure. They can find enjoyment in appalling situations because those situations are associated with the rewarding experience of the substance-induced high.

The psychological process of association is also responsible for two common aspects of addiction: triggers and cravings. As applied to addiction, a trigger is a mental cue that produces thoughts about a particular substance or experience. Triggers may be sensory (sights, sounds, smells, and so on), verbal (a word or phrase that is somehow associated with the substance), or emotional. A craving is an overwhelming desire for that substance or experience.

Triggers and cravings are common to the human experience, as anyone who has ever been on a diet knows. Seeing a food commercial on television, smelling certain odors, even driving past a favorite restaurant can weaken our resolve to eat less. I was once traveling with a friend who had a weakness for sweets. As we passed an A&W root beer stand, he commented that A&W made the best root beer floats in the world. I suggested that we stop so he could buy one, but he declined. He was "watching his weight." Forty or so miles later, as night was falling, he said he recalled passing a motel a few miles back. We turned around and eventually found ourselves at the A&W stand, where he ordered a large float. The thought of that float had been on his mind for more than an hour and had finally proven irresistible.

Triggers seem to be a feature of human psychology from an early age, as we can see from the effectiveness of advertising that targets children. When children enter a store, they are drawn to food, toys, and other items they have seen in commercials, because they have learned to associate those items with pleasure. When a Scooby-Doo movie was released when my grandson was little, he excitedly pointed out every promotional poster and billboard we passed, things I would not have noticed if he hadn't been with me. Evidently, he associated Scooby-Doo with fun—with pleasure.

Triggers evoke stored memories of special meaning. What triggers a reaction or a craving in one person may be completely meaningless to another. When I bought my daughter a pair of sneakers early in her recovery, she pointed out that the slogan on the box read "Get the addiction," a phrase I had overlooked. She also asked me about a cardboard box on my closet shelf that was printed with images of syringes. The box had come from a clinic where one of my other children had worked, and it contained an old china tea set. I had never noticed the images before because they had no meaning for me.

The difficulty for addicts is that triggers can be almost anything, and the resulting cravings can be particularly intense. Places and people associated with getting high are obvious triggers. However, many are not so easily predictable.

One addict described hearing a siren one day, which reminded him of the ringing sensation in his head that had often accompanied the rush of cocaine. "It was a head rush, like an electric shock through my whole body," he said. "All of a sudden I just wanted it so bad."

An alcoholic described her feelings when passing a liquor store or seeing a beer commercial: "You get weak. You can taste it. You want it so bad it's unreal."

A young woman recalled seeing a stranger who was wearing a blue blouse. She said, "My mind went from the color blue to my old jean jacket to shooting up in about half a second, and I was soon thinking, 'Okay—I'm gonna go out and cop, and I'm gonna do this and that,' all in a second. Your mind just goes there."

A young man recalled watching a Fourth of July parade from the porch of a halfway house. He said, "One of the marchers had a mustache like a buddy I used to get high with. I started to shake. I had to go inside before I went out and scored some dope."

Emotions, sometimes barely perceived, can also trigger intense cravings. The mind senses boredom, loneliness, guilt, fear, anxiety, or other distressing feelings and instantly identifies the remedy as alcohol or other drugs.

One woman described a painful breakup of an important relationship by saying, "There was this lump in my throat, like my heart was in my throat. I knew that if I did a bag of dope, the lump would go away."

Ironically, happy feelings can also trigger cravings because the greedy brain wants to intensify the good feelings. The logic might go something like this: "I feel good now, and by smoking a little dope, I'll feel even better." It's the same thinking that causes many people to eat to excess: "One cookie makes me feel good. If I eat a dozen, I'll feel even better." The brain selectively forgets the negative feelings that usually result from binges and recalls only the immediate reward.

Triggers and cravings, conditioned responses that stem from the psychological phenomenon of association, are common to all human beings. But association is not the only influence that psychology has on addiction. Another major influence is "self-talk": the messages that addicts, like all people, tell themselves.

A well-established view of the human experience is that most of us live up to or down to our own self-image. That is, our beliefs about ourselves play a tremendous role in determining our path in life. If we believe we are deserving and capable, we are likely to make choices that are in our best interest. If we believe we are not worthy, we are likely to make choices that fulfill that belief. Addicts are not exempt from this principle. Their self-talk and "stinking thinking" are apt to include messages that prolong and deepen their addiction.

Jane recalled some of her own self-talk during her period of deepest addiction: "I always believed in God, but I just thought God made all sorts of people. I was simply one of those people, a junkie that God made. That's what I thought: 'God said you will always be a drug addict.' I'd already given my kids up, and I accepted it."

She went on to describe the feeling of hopelessness that often accompanies addiction: "You get to a point when you're using where you say, 'Fuck it.' I looked at all the damage I had done and I thought, 'There's no way I can fix this.' I was shooting everything under the sun because I couldn't fix what I had damaged."

Jane said that she would act tough and tell people that she liked the way she was, but she added, "Inside I hated myself; I wanted to die." Lia recalled, "I always felt like shit." Mark said, "I was disgusting, and I knew it. But I couldn't change, so I drank even more."

Despite the bravado that many addicts display, most of them are filled with shame. Shame goes much deeper than guilt. Guilt tells us that we've *done* something wrong. It's about an action that can be addressed. Shame tells us that we *are* fundamentally wrong. It says that our essential being, our very *self,* is fatally flawed, inadequate, and unworthy of love. My own daughter confessed that, even well into recovery, she secretly hated herself and felt utterly worthless. She habitually called herself names—stupid, ugly, garbage, loser—and believed without question that she was unworthy of love or respect or happiness. This level of shame goes far deeper than poor self-esteem. This is the soul-destroying shame born of self-loathing—the shame that makes the oblivion of addiction so alluring and the struggle for recovery so formidable.

Shame is emotionally crippling, making addicts believe that they're bad or weak or hopeless and that they don't deserve a better life. What's more, their attempts at recovery are often hampered by a complex set of factors that led them down the path of addiction in the first place. In the next chapter, we'll look at some of those factors.

FOUR

Who Gets Addicted?

"An addict is someone who seeks physical solutions to emotional or spiritual problems."
—Carolyn Knapp

As we saw in the last chapter, the disease of addiction changes the way the brain functions, both physically and psychologically. But these changes don't tell the whole story. After all, plenty of people drink alcohol, experiment with drugs, or take prescribed painkillers without getting addicted. A more perplexing question is, Why do some people become addicted while others don't? Research provides some answers, starting with the role of genetics.

While no specific "addiction gene" has yet been discovered, research suggests that some people are genetically prone to addiction. In fact, the likelihood of developing an addiction is 50 to 75 percent higher in those with a family history of the disease. This does not mean that addiction is inherited. It means that the vulnerability to addiction can be passed from one generation to the next.

Jane said that she grew up in a home where alcohol and other drugs were never present. She could find no genetic basis for her condition until she learned as an adult that the father who had raised her was not her biological father. "I was going through my mother's stuff and found some photographs of my mother with another man," she said. "She told me she divorced him because he was an abusive alcoholic. After that, he just kind of disappeared into the street life. I look just like him and probably inherited the addiction gene from him."

In my daughter's case, the genetic vulnerability to addiction was inherited from both parents. Her father is an alcoholic, her father's sister was a heroin addict, her paternal grandmother was addicted to "pep pills," and her paternal grandfather was an alcoholic (as were his brothers). One of my sisters was addicted to amphetamines, my father and both grandfathers were alcoholics, and my maternal grandmother was addicted to codeine, an opium derivative.

It's likely that part of my daughter's genetic inheritance includes a vulnerability to addiction, much as the vulnerability to certain cancers or heart disease can be inherited. This is consistent with the belief expressed by many people in recovery that they were "born addicts." "I was always an alcoholic and addict—always—and the painkillers triggered the addiction," said one man whose twin knee operations precipitated more than ten years of drug addiction.

Some addicts explain their condition as an "allergy" that makes their response to alcohol or other drugs fundamentally different from that of "nonallergic" people. Certainly, many addicts' early experiences with substances seem to be especially powerful, meaningful, and profound, leading to an emotional connection that they tend to describe in the language of lovers: "It was what I was waiting for my whole life." "It was what I'd always been looking for." "Oh my God, I was in my glory." "I couldn't get enough of it."

Such powerful responses may be symptomatic of genetic differences between those who become addicted and those who don't.

Environment

Environment also plays a significant role in who does or does not become addicted. Home, community, and peer groups influence our attitudes toward most things, including substances of abuse. If our social group strongly discourages the use of alcohol or other drugs, we're less likely to try them than is someone whose social group tolerates or even models their use.

When my children were growing up, alcohol was part of daily life. My husband and I drank beer or wine almost every evening, and alcohol figured prominently in most family gatherings. I found nothing remarkable about any of this at the time. In hindsight, I see that my daughter learned early that substance use is acceptable and even normal. (The fact that her siblings do not have substance use disorder suggests that they did not inherit the genetic vulnerability to addiction.)

In addition to family behaviors and attitudes, social norms influence our beliefs about alcohol and other drugs. Nowadays, teens in all U.S. communities, from major cities to small towns, have access to all the major addictive drugs. Many kids have been offered alcohol or other drugs by age thirteen. And pop culture exposes kids to countless images of drug and alcohol use, often sending the message that substance use is not only acceptable. It's cool.

Age

One of the most striking predictors of future addiction is the age at which substance use begins. Around 80 percent of addicted adults began abusing substances before age eighteen, a statistic suggesting that the teenage brain may be more susceptible to addiction than the adult brain.

One reason for this may be that teen brains have less of the fatty substance called myelin than do adult brains. Myelin acts like an insulator as messages travel from one neuron to another. The less myelin we have, the more intense those messages tend to be. This explains why teens—whose brains are still "in progress"—actually experience more intense sensations of pleasure and pain than do adults. Researchers at Hazelden Betty Ford suggest, "This means that teens may crave the alleviation of negative emotions more urgently than adults, because these emotions are truly felt more deeply. It also means that when teens engage in risky behaviors like alcohol and other drug use, the reward pathway of the teen brain is highly sensitive to substances' effects."

Another reason for teens' vulnerability to addiction is the fact that the prefrontal cortex—the area of the brain that governs judgment, problem-solving, and self-control—doesn't fully develop until around age twenty-five. This explains teenagers' penchant for risk-taking and their belief in their own invincibility. "It won't happen to me" is a common theme. But as alcohol and other drugs alter brain chemistry, school, hobbies, goals, family, and nonusing friends fall by the wayside. In an ominous reflection of the changing brain, the developing addict is increasingly motivated by just one thing: to re-experience the incredible pleasure of the early chemical highs.

Emotional and Mental Health Disorders

Approximately 9.2 million adults in the United States have co-occurring disorders; that is, they have both a mental health and a substance use disorder, according to the Substance Abuse and Mental Health Services Administration's (SAMHSA) 2018 National Survey on Drug Use and Health.

People with depression, anxiety, and other emotional and mental health disorders are about twice as likely as the general population to develop substance use disorder. For those individuals, substances offer relief from emotional pain, a way to "self-medicate" that's profoundly compelling.

The author Carolyn Knapp noted in her autobiography, *Drinking: A Love Story,* that many people who become addicted struggle with painful feelings of fear, emptiness, loneliness, and self-loathing before they start abusing substances. She wrote, "Most alcoholics I know experience that hunger long before they pick up the first drink, that yearning for something, something outside the self that will provide relief and solace and well-being. You hear echoes of it all the time in AA meetings, that sense that there's a well of emptiness inside and that the trick in sobriety is to find new ways to fill it, spiritual ways instead of physical ones."

Bert Pepper, MD, a public health physician and psychiatrist who served on SAMHSA's advisory board, echoed that observation. He noted in an interview, "More than 60 percent of people with bipolar disorder have drug and/or alcohol problems, and the percentage for people with schizophrenia is even higher. And although the fifty-year-old alcoholic may have become addicted as a result of too many liquid lunches, 60 percent or more of young adult addiction patients have preexisting emotional, family, or psychiatric problems. So many adolescents have emotional needs that don't get attended to, and so they self-medicate."

He went on to say that "the early development of anxiety, depression, thinking problems, and behavior problems, when compounded by the early use of drugs and alcohol, interferes with the development of a mature, stable, functional personality and sense of self."

The journey to adulthood is complicated for most of us, but it's especially challenging for young people who struggle with emotional and mental health disorders. Substance use makes the process even harder, sabotaging the development of effective life skills and crippling the potential for personal growth.

Pepper identifies behaviors that are typical of people with co-occurring disorders as follows: low frustration tolerance, lying to avoid punishment, hostile dependency (exhibiting hostility toward those whose help they rely on), limit-testing (normal in children but problematic in later adolescence and adulthood), alexithymia (the inability to verbalize feelings or ask for help), rejection sensitivity (an extreme need to be accepted), dualistic thinking (judging people and events as only right or wrong, good or bad, without accepting moderation or shades of gray), and present-tense thinking (lacking a sense of past or future, leading to repetition of the same mistakes over and over again).

Many of the parents I have spoken with about their child's addiction support these findings. They say their child was depressed, anxious, or oversensitive before the substance abuse began. My own daughter certainly falls into this category. I remember asking a counselor early in my daughter's rehabilitation why some people get addicted while others don't. She said that there is no definitive answer but "parents often remember that there was something just a little different, a little out-of-step about the child even before the addiction began."

Dr. DuPont adds a set of traits he defines as "character disorder" to the list of mental health problems that increase someone's risk of becoming addicted. In *The Selfish Brain,* he writes, "The most prominent features of character disorder are thinking about the present rather than the future and frequent dishonesty. Other features include relative insensitivity to the feelings of others, rebellion against authority, and relative imperviousness to punishment."

The personal histories of many addicts support his observations. One twenty-one-year-old alcoholic recalled, "I was this rebellious kid right from the beginning. I was always getting grounded. I was bad in school. I didn't get good grades. I was always a risk-taker. I mean, at five years old I would jump off anything. I'd jump into the biggest waves at the beach, swim out deeper than anyone else. I can't remember ever having fear. I think I was also an angry child. I don't know what to blame it on, but there were times I was definitely angry at my family. I don't really know why. I definitely had a chip on my shoulder."

A twenty-five-year-old heroin addict said, "I was always lying to my parents. One time when they thought I was going to school, I got on a plane and flew two thousand miles away. I did whatever I wanted, no matter what they did to me."

A forty-one-year-old alcoholic remembered running away from home when she was fourteen and dropping out of school at sixteen despite her parents' anger: "They were really hurt, but I didn't care. It didn't matter."

My own daughter was deceitful, rebellious, and stubborn long before she became addicted. For example, when she was twelve, I dropped her and a friend off at a neighborhood movie theater. Instead of going to the movie, they managed to buy cigarettes and smoked the entire pack even though it made them feel deathly ill. At fourteen she began to violate my privacy by wearing (and often ruining) my clothes despite my repeated objections. When she was fifteen, she stole one of my spare car keys and gave it to an older friend so they could drive around in my car without my knowledge. She also started skipping school, precipitating countless meetings with counselors to try to get her back on track—to no avail.

Of course, rebelliousness, shortsightedness, and the desire to avoid consequences are typical traits of many teenagers (and adults). Not everyone who exhibits character disorder becomes addicted. Nevertheless, many budding addicts do seem to have severe difficulty planning for the future, relating to the feelings of others, and learning from consequences. Addiction exacerbates these characteristics. It is also possible that character disorder is a manifestation of the mental or emotional disorders that are so common among the addicted population.

The Reckless Pursuit of Pleasure

The consequences of addiction are far-reaching, hindering normal brain development and creating long-lasting problems with problem-solving, decision-making, and impulse control. Moreover, addiction halts the maturation process and short-circuits the fundamental task of building a sense of self.

None of us come into the world knowing who we are. Instead, we build our personal identity through a long process of trial and error—discovering our likes and dislikes, testing our strengths and weaknesses, and exploring our dreams and fears. Addiction limits life experiences to a narrow, repetitive cycle of getting and using substances. In the process, it numbs the thoughts, feelings, and insights that lead to self-discovery, shutting the door on personal growth.

Without a secure sense of self to provide inner stability, addicts are subject to the ever-increasing demands of the addicted brain. As the disease progresses, it can push them into appalling, life-threatening choices, behaviors, and situations that mirror their deep inner distress.

Mark recalled that, at the height of his active alcoholism, he was more than eighty pounds overweight, his eyes were always bloodshot, his sweat reeked of alcohol, and he felt sick to the point of exhaustion. Still, he could not stop drinking.

Jane continued to solicit sex to support her habit, even when a serial killer was known to be murdering prostitutes in her town.

Lia, who followed a popular band's concert tours around the country, described having no fear in a number of perilous situations: "I've walked through every single ghetto across this country with acid in one pocket [to sell] and needles in another. I'd be scared about getting arrested so I'd be looking out for cops, but I'd walk up to a crack house, a dope house, with my money on me. Sometimes when I bought drugs, I'd try it right there, to make sure it's real. One time, I woke up in a crack house where I didn't know anybody. But I really didn't have any fear."

That the addicted brain loses its power to recognize danger became clear to me when my daughter described attending the funeral of a heroin addict who had died of an overdose. I asked if seeing the effects of heroin had frightened her into wanting to get clean. She calmly replied, "Mom, when addicts hear that someone has OD'd, they think, 'That must have been good stuff. Where can I get some?'"

She also told me that her boyfriend had OD'd several times, and she described one scene in some detail: "We had just shot up, and I was nodding on the couch. For some reason I opened my eyes, and I saw him facedown on the floor. I called 911. They came, gave him a shot, and took him to the emergency room. If I hadn't opened my eyes, he would have died."

Another addict, who OD'd many times, described one such incident: "My friends had shot me full of saltwater, because that's supposed to bring you back, but it didn't. So they called 911. The EMTs were working on me when I came to. I thought,

'No, no.' They were wrecking my high, and I wanted them to leave me alone. They took me to the hospital anyway. I was so high I gave them my home address, so my mom got the emergency room bill. Usually I would've given a fake address."

Those experiences didn't stop any of these addicts from continuing their drug use. Their addicted brains had ceased to be tools for survival and had become mere instruments of pleasure and escape—at any cost.

Ironically, as addiction progresses and the meaning of life is reduced to the reckless pursuit of pleasure, an addict's life almost invariably becomes one of unremitting misery. Problems multiply, losses mount, and the physical, emotional, and spiritual toll becomes enormous.

"I could clear a room just by walking into it," Mark recalled. "Nobody wanted to be around me."

Jane remembered living with her children in "a cute little house with ridiculously low rent" and being evicted for not paying rent because all her money was going for drugs. She also remembered how drugs changed her relationship with her boyfriend: "When we were first together, he didn't want me working the streets. He didn't like that. At the end, he'd tell me to go out and make some money."

Most painful to Jane is remembering the effect her addiction had on her children, who spent most of their childhood with her mother. She recalled, "So for two years I'm a maintenance heroin addict, doing two bags a day. Then I meet this guy who shows me how to steal. He'd go into a store and steal, and I'd bring it back for cash. Now I'm shooting ten bags a day, and my kids are starting to interfere because I have to feed them, bathe them, and stop and let them play. One day I left them with a babysitter, packed up my whole house into a U-Haul, and took off for Florida with my boyfriend."

Jane devoted most of the next six years to drug use, with frequent stints in jail and halfway houses. Sometimes she was wracked by guilt, but even this couldn't make her stop: "So now I'm living with the guilt of leaving my kids. I thought about them all the time. One time when my son's birthday came up, I was sitting in a shooting gallery saying, 'Today is my son's birthday. Today is the most important day in my life, when I gave birth to this human being.' I'd remember all that and I'd sob and sob, then shoot more dope. I wanted to kill myself. I kept saying, 'How could I do this to my kids?' But I couldn't stop."

Lia, too, suffered deeply because of her addiction. She said: "One time I was in this halfway house and people were talking about prostitution, and I could not even envision it. Never in my wildest dreams. No way in hell. You know what I mean? It just was not in my vision. I couldn't picture how that could happen, because when I was dope sick before, that would never even enter my mind. The first thing I would think about was stealing, conning, or manipulating, getting money somehow, but I wouldn't do that. That's the scary part, because it was unreal to me. But it kind of just happened.

"I was dope sick and really needed money, and I just started doing it. You're numb; there's no feeling at all. I didn't even care. I'd tell myself, 'I'm getting money for it. There's nothing romantic about this. It's just a job.'

"The more I did it, the more I had to use. I was shooting heroin and cocaine all the time. My head was always hanging down when I was with my real friends. I felt numb. One day my boyfriend and I got in this huge fight. He wasn't making any money. I was supplying the money and the drugs. Before he went to sleep, he told me to save him some dope, but I used it all, so he flushed my needles down the toilet. We were screaming at each other, and we each had a champagne bottle in our hands, ready to hit each other. We just stopped and sort of gasped, 'Oh my God' and started to cry. I looked around our house, with pizza boxes in one corner, ashes in another, a TV on cardboard boxes, spoons and needles in the kitchen, crack on the stove.

"That was a moment of clarity for me. I didn't want to live like that anymore, always fighting over money and drugs. In the beginning, our relationship wasn't about drugs."

Broken relationships, poor health, destitution, and emotional and spiritual bankruptcy: these are the terrible price that many addicts pay over the course of their addiction, until some internal awakening—a moment of clarity or of grace—interrupts the progression of the disease.

Confronting the Beast

The medical and scientific communities have made many advances in understanding the disease of addiction. But many questions remain. Why, for example, do some addicts seek recovery after a relatively mild encounter with negative consequences while others suffer repeated traumatic losses and still continue to use? Why do some addicts find recovery after completing only one treatment program while others enter rehab many times before recovery truly takes hold?

The answers to these and other questions remain locked in the human psyche. What we do know is that addiction is a destructive, progressive disease that carries devastating consequences—both for addicts and for their families.

We also know that no one can cure an addict and that addicts must be fully responsible for finding and maintaining their own recovery. Nevertheless, a family can have a positive influence on an addicted loved one, even if that person does not live with or have much interaction with the family. They can do this by acting as role models for healthy living and by creating an environment that promotes recovery and personal growth.

As a first step in creating a healthy, recovery-friendly environment, families must become aware of and change their own unhealthy behaviors that have likely developed in response to their loved one's addiction.

FIVE

Addicted to the Addict

"Be not angry that you cannot make others
as you wish them to be, since you cannot
make yourself as you wish to be."
—THOMAS À KEMPIS

CELESTE WILL NEVER FORGET the moment she learned that her only son was addicted to heroin. His ex-girlfriend had hinted that he had a drug problem. Celeste was afraid to approach the question directly, and when her son, a twenty-nine-year-old electrician, denied there was anything wrong, Celeste dropped the matter. But she herself had begun to observe some disturbing changes. When her son came to visit, he would flop on the couch as if he had no energy. Although he worked as hard as ever, he was usually short of money. He had lost weight, and his clothes no longer fit. He seemed listless and depressed.

After weeks of nagging, Celeste finally convinced her son to let her take him to a clinic for an evaluation. She recalled the events that followed: "A psychiatrist and a drug counselor met with each of us separately, then called us both in together. That's when the reality of the whole thing really hit me: he was using drugs and had been for a long time. I was sitting in a room with these two people and my son, and all of this was coming out. I was shaking from head to toe. I couldn't control the shaking and I felt absolute panic. It was as though I was just informed of the most horrible thing I could possibly imagine.

"My son was sitting there beside me, and they were trying to convince him that he needed to go into treatment. He was very defensive and kept saying he could do it on his own. At one point he reached over and grabbed my hand. It was clammy wet. The psychiatrist said to him, 'Look at her. Look what it's doing to her. She can't stop shaking.'

"Then the drug counselor said, 'He's not concerned right now about how you feel. All he cares about is how he's going to get his next fix. If he continues on this path, a year from now he will be in jail or dead.' She made it clear to me what shape my son was in. I couldn't comprehend the reality of what she was saying to me. I said, 'You don't understand, I'm just finding out about this tonight for the first time. I had no idea about what was going on.' I think I came close to passing out. It was as though my blood had been drained."

I experienced a similar sensation when I discovered that my daughter was addicted to heroin. I had been worried about her for months, even years, as she lost jobs, got evicted from apartments, and became ever more reclusive. My fears came to a head one night as I drove past her apartment house. Her roommates had been threatening to throw her out, and I wondered if they actually had. I spotted her parked car on a side street and saw blankets, pillows, and some kitchen items piled in back. My heart began to race. She was almost certainly living in her car.

I waited by the car for a while and then returned to the apartment house. I leaned on the buzzer, determined not to leave until I had some answers. "I want to find out what's happened to my daughter," I said through the intercom. Reluctantly, her roommates let me in. I could see that they were uncomfortable, maybe even embarrassed. I asked if they knew where she was and why they had forced her to leave. They mumbled some words that didn't make much sense. I kept pressing for details, and finally one of them looked at me and said, "Do you know your daughter's a heroin addict?"

I remember grabbing a chair for support as the floor seemed to collapse under me. Everything became fuzzy and far away. I could barely breathe. "How do you know?" I demanded.

I wanted proof, although I didn't doubt the truth of what I had heard. The young woman before me was merely confirming what I had feared on some level for a long time. She went into details about my daughter, describing bloody tissues, nodding off at the kitchen table, and arms covered with scabs. I could barely take it in. I felt nauseated and terrified. Among the horrible images that crowded my mind, one thought rose to the top: I had to find my daughter and help her.

I returned to her car and waited in the shadows. After a long time, a small white car full of young men pulled up and dropped off my daughter before driving away. A dim streetlight lit the way as she approached her car. She looked terrible. Her short, dyed-red hair was matted flat to her head on one side, as if she had been sleeping. One of her heavily drawn-on eyebrows had worn off, giving her a lopsided look. She wore short shorts and a long-sleeved T-shirt.

I stepped out of the shadows and called her name. She gave me a sleepy, quizzical smile and asked what I was doing there. With a shaking voice I told her what I had learned. "Show me your arms," I demanded. She backed away. "Mom, you're psychotic!" she screeched. "I haven't done anything wrong! You're psychotic!"

"Show me your arms!" I insisted.

She turned and bolted. I chased after her through narrow streets in a neighborhood that some women were afraid of even in daylight. "I'm never going to stop!" I called. "You're either coming home with me, or we'll see a cop and I'll have you arrested! Those are your choices!" I felt strong saying that, believing I had taken charge of the situation. All her problems could be fixed now that I was taking matters into my own hands.

We ran for several blocks until she abruptly gave up and became quite passive. She returned willingly to my car. As I drove her home, we said little. I remember telling her to go to bed. We'd talk about things in the morning, I said, as if she were twelve years old. As if I would come up with a solution overnight, and tomorrow everything would be all right.

I had no way of knowing the struggles that lay ahead or the seriousness of my daughter's situation. I did not know that I was about to join millions of American families whose lives are turned upside down by addiction. And I could not have imagined that my own behavior—like that of so many families— would come to mirror the disease of addiction itself.

Just as addiction is characterized by denial, obsession with drugs, compulsion to use, and emotional and physical illness, family members experience denial, obsession with the addict, compulsion to control the addict, and emotional and physical illness. In a very real sense, families can become addicted to the addict. Like all addictions, the process begins with denial.

A Game Called Denial

Most families, when describing their first awareness of a loved one's addiction, admit that they'd known there was something wrong for a very long time. "All the signs were there, but we didn't want to see them," they say. "There were all these red flags that we didn't pay attention to." "I kept telling myself it wasn't possible, but I wasn't surprised when I found out."

A father recalled, "When I look back, there were a lot of little things. My son would stop by the house and say, 'Dad, do you have ten bucks I could borrow?' Everything in his house was so disorganized, so slovenly, and he was never like that.

Everything used to be neat and organized, and his bills were paid on time. I remember telling myself he was depressed because his girlfriend had broken up with him."

One woman said that for more than a year she counted empty bottles in her sister's trash cans every time she went to visit, all the while telling herself that everything was fine. "When my husband would suggest that my sister had a drinking problem, I'd become furious with him. It was easier to pretend than to face the truth," she said.

A young man recalled that his parents' alcoholism dominated much of his childhood, but nobody ever mentioned it: "We could never go to a restaurant that didn't serve beer, not even for lunch. Neither of them thought twice about driving drunk, even with us kids in the car. They'd drink every night and usually wind up in a huge fight. My brother and I would go upstairs and try not to listen. Both of us left home at the age of seventeen. But to this day, my brother refuses to believe our parents are alcoholics."

Being aware of the signs of addiction but refusing to see their significance is quite common among family members who are in denial. I remember being very aware that my daughter always wore long sleeves, even in extremely hot weather, and telling myself it didn't mean anything. I noticed her boyfriend nodding off in restaurants at least twice and told myself that he must have an illness, maybe narcolepsy.

I talked to a friend who was an alcohol and drug counselor and described my daughter's constant lack of money, her reluctance to spend time with me, and her extreme lethargy. "Sounds like heroin to me," my friend said.

"Oh, no. She would never do that," I replied.

Just as denial allows addicts to avoid facing their addiction, it enables families to avoid confronting the problem. As long as the addiction is not acknowledged, families and addicts can carry on as if nothing is wrong. Everyone gets to pretend that things are normal, and no one has to experience the discomfort or fear that comes with facing a difficult situation head-on. It's a lot like the elephant in the room, the one that nobody wants to talk about. Everyone knows it's there, but the whole family makes believe it isn't.

Even after families have accepted that their loved one is addicted to alcohol or other drugs, denial is likely to persist. They may deny the depth of the problem and refuse to acknowledge its destructive effects. "I know she uses heroin, but she'd never shoot up," they may say. "Everyone fools around with cocaine. It's what kids do nowadays." "It's only prescription drugs. It's not like she's really an addict." "He's not a hard-core alcoholic. He only drinks beer." "I know he's using again, but he still has his job so it can't be that bad."

By denying the seriousness of the problem, families join their loved one in the game of pretending that things "aren't that bad"—as if there were some acceptable level of addiction. It's a comforting thought that ignores the fact that addiction is a chronic, progressive disease that always gets worse until something intervenes to halt its progress.

Perhaps most damaging to families is their denial of the effects of addiction on themselves. Since addiction stunts emotional growth and keeps an addict's focus solely on self-gratification, addicts are prone to trampling all over other people's property, boundaries, and emotions. Loving family members may have trouble seeing what is taking place or may minimize the addict's transgressions. They may allow themselves to be manipulated, lied to, and taken advantage of over and over again, often with the mistaken belief that they are helping the addict.

For example, Jim, a small-appliance mechanic whose brother was addicted to alcohol, crack cocaine, and amphetamines, began to notice that whenever his brother paid him a visit, a small item or sum of cash would go missing. He explained, "It would be something like a gold chain that I hadn't worn in a long time, so I'd think maybe I misplaced it. Or I'd have ten dollars less in my wallet than I thought I'd had and figured I must have spent it somewhere. One day my watch was gone, and that's when I put it all together. He'd been stealing from me for weeks, but I didn't want to see it."

Hope recalled that after each visit by her heroin-addicted daughter, something would be missing from the house. "I was so grateful to see her, to know she was at least alive, that I pretended not to notice," she said. "Besides, we were raising her children at that time, and I felt it was good for them to have some contact with their mother." Facing a no-win situation, Hope started leaving a twenty-dollar bill on the table "so she wouldn't have to steal."

Another mother, Audrey, said that her son used to steal money from her pocketbook "all the time," but she stopped confronting him about it because he was so convincing in his denial. He also stole his father's tools and just about anything else of value he could find. "But there wasn't much that we could do about it," she said, "other than throw him out, and then his addiction might have gotten even worse."

Overlooking an addict's thefts and dishonesty is fairly common among families in the early stages of dealing with addiction. It's easier for families to ignore the transgressions than to confront the addict, who always has a plausible excuse at hand. When the addict says, "I'm going to the store for cigarettes" and returns high three hours later, family members may pretend they have been told the truth. When the obviously impaired addict says, "I haven't used any drugs or had anything to drink," family members may try to convince themselves that the addict is merely overtired. I remember seeing a small drop of blood, an obvious puncture site, on a vein on my daughter's hand one night, and asking her what it was. "I burned myself with a cigarette," she said offhandedly. I knew it wasn't a burn, but I tried to convince myself that she was telling the truth.

The problem with denial is that—just as addicts exist in an alternate world—we ourselves begin to lose touch with reality. When we try to convince ourselves that what we see, believe, and feel is not real, we start to question the validity of our own perceptions. In time, the lines between reality and make-believe may blur.

"I felt I owed it to my husband to drive him to and from his counseling appointments," said one woman, "because he was at least trying to get help for his problems." She was able to overlook the fact that the counselor was easily accessible by bus and that her husband usually managed to obtain drugs during the interval between her dropping him off and picking him up. Typically, he was insensible for two or three days following his appointments.

One woman recalled waiting in her car outside a pawnshop for almost an hour while her son went in to sell some possessions. "I felt dirty sitting there, like I was doing something seedy or distasteful," she said. "But he had to sell things to pay the rent because he'd lost his job. At least that's what he told me, and I wanted to help him out."

I personally signed loans for three cars for my daughter, each of which she managed to destroy while under the influence of alcohol or other drugs. I told myself that she was a victim of bad luck, that she needed a car to get to work, and that she was trying really hard to overcome her addiction. I pretended not to notice when she came home almost unable to speak.

Denial can lead to an enormous amount of unhappiness for families as they struggle to sustain a version of reality that on some level they know is false. They suppress their suspicions, their pain, their fears, and their sense that they are somehow being "had"—that the addict is using them. Yet families may persist in their denial for a very long time because they don't know what else to do.

Obsessed with the Addict

In the early stages of denial, families may be able to overlook the addict's erratic behavior, thereby avoiding the stress of facing addiction. Eventually, however, the progressive nature of the disease makes it impossible to ignore, and loving families and friends are likely to find themselves increasingly disturbed by the changes they see. Even if they are still in the throes of denial, families may spend a tremendous amount of time worrying about their loved one. They may drag the addict to doctors and counselors, spend long hours discussing the person with friends and family members, and repeatedly try to persuade their loved one to reveal "what is wrong."

I spent years fretting about my daughter's obvious mental health problems (and denying that they had anything to do with addiction). I would often walk by the apartment where she lived with her boyfriend, hoping to get a glimpse of her so I would know she was all right. I usually didn't ring their doorbell, because she had made it clear that she didn't want me interfering in her life, but I was so preoccupied with her that I was repeatedly drawn to her neighborhood.

I also discussed her constantly with my other children, my closest friends, and anyone else who would listen. No matter what the initial topic of conversation, I would find some way to bring it around to my daughter. (Looking back, I'm surprised that anyone was willing to talk to me after a while!) Once, a friend pulled his car over to the side of the road because I had burst into tears and was sobbing uncontrollably for no reason that I could articulate, other than vague fears about my daughter.

Predictably, once the veil of denial was lifted and the depth of her addiction fully revealed, my preoccupation turned into full-blown obsession. She was rarely out of my mind, and my entire life became centered on her. I seemed to always have a knot of fear in my stomach. Social activities lost their appeal. I found no pleasure in anything. I cried for hours on end, and obsessive thoughts circled in my head like a gerbil on a wheel: Why had this happened? What had I done wrong? What was going to become of her? How could I make her stop?

Others experience similar responses to a loved one's addiction. The wife of a heroin addict said that she worried about her husband constantly. "He'd been clean for years when we got married, but about three years later, he confessed that he had relapsed," she said. "I started watching him like a hawk. Every time he stepped out the door, I'd feel this panic, thinking he was probably going out to score. Sometimes I'd be out driving around at eleven or twelve at night, looking for his car. I remember so many times sitting in the kitchen in the middle of the night calling every single hospital and police station I could think of to see if he'd been in an accident or OD'd. My whole world was consumed with fear for his safety and trying to make him get well."

"My mood depends on how well she's doing," observed a mother of an alcoholic. "I can gauge her state of mind within five seconds of seeing her or talking to her on the phone. If things are going okay, I can feel my mood lighten. If she's not having a good day, my spirits sink. It's like we're attached at the hip. When she cycles up, I cycle up. When she cycles down, I cycle down."

The father of a cocaine addict said of his son, "His addiction is the biggest thing in my world right now. I think about it day and night. My other kids and my wife hardly even exist anymore. There's no room for them in my head." He could have added that there was also no room for himself in his head.

As obsession deepens, family members may lose their sense of personal identity. It's as if their own lives cease to have any value, and their state of being is determined by what is going on in the addict's life rather than by what is going on in their own. They put personal goals, interests, and pleasures to the side, and their very existence seems meaningful only when it is related to the addict. If the addict is doing well, they do well; if the addict is struggling, they struggle. Even everyday experiences may be filtered through thoughts of the addict: "If only he could see this sunset, it might reawaken his appreciation of life." "If only she were here to see the baby, she might realize how much she is missing." "This is such a good movie. I know he'd get a lot out of it if I could just convince him to see it."

As obsession with the addict blossoms, its close counterpart—compulsion—is likely to unfurl. Because the family member's peace of mind is so dependent on the addict's condition, it becomes imperative that their loved one be "cured." As time goes on, finding a cure becomes important not only for the addict's benefit, but for the health and happiness of the well-meaning family member.

More often than not, the urge to cure the addict leads to a grim determination to take control.

The Compulsion to Control

The first counselor I consulted about my daughter's addiction told me, "Control is the flip side of fear." I remembered that often as my efforts to control my daughter's behavior and cure her addiction led me to behave in ways that once would have seemed unthinkable.

I had never been a particularly controlling mother. In my daughter's teenage years, I respected her privacy, never searched her personal belongings, and (foolishly) trusted her to make sound choices. All of that changed when I learned of her addiction. Suddenly, her business was my business. I became determined to monitor her every move.

She came home to live with me after I'd found her living in her car. It was a move that I welcomed in the belief that I could help her. The fear that my daughter would die was never far from my consciousness. I got in the habit of tiptoeing downstairs in the early morning when she was still asleep. I'd bend close to her face to make sure she was breathing. I tried to listen to her phone conversations, and on more than one occasion I lay on the kitchen floor with my ear pressed to the grate when she was on the phone downstairs. I searched her drawers, looked behind furniture and under her mattress, and felt along the tops of the tiles in the suspended ceiling. I went through her car early in the morning as she slept. I examined her clothing for evidence of blood spots or burn holes. I checked up on her whereabouts by calling her counselor's office or prospective employers. (Had she kept her counseling appointment? Had she gone for that job interview?) Since our voices are similar on the phone, I was not above calling people and pretending to be her. Once I met with a private detective to discuss the possibility of having her followed and was only deterred by a sense of shame.

I did these things in an effort to control my daughter's addiction and save her from herself. The harder I tried to save her, the more obsessed I became. My story is all too common among families of addicts.

Eventually, the compulsion to cure the addiction leads to the compulsion to control just about every aspect of the addict's life, including treatment plans, finances, housing, jobs, relationships, nutrition, exercise, health care, grooming, clothes, hobbies, attitudes, values, and even feelings. Well-intentioned family members believe that if they can get the addict properly treated and appropriately situated, the addiction will go away. They are apt to use every means at their disposal to persuade the addict to agree to their plans, sometimes employing well-worn techniques of manipulation:

Guilt	"If you loved me, you wouldn't do this."
Threats	"I'll throw you out if you don't do what I want."
Shame	"You're disgusting. How can you even live with yourself?"
Bribery	"I'll pay your rent for a year if you do what I ask."
Rage	"I hate you! I don't ever want to see you again."
Tears	"You're breaking my heart."
Reasoning	"If you buy drugs instead of paying your rent, you'll become homeless."

These attempts at manipulation and control never work, for the simple reason that it's not in our power to force anyone to change. Change is an internal process that happens only when someone is ready for it. Still, in our desperation, most of us grapple with a compulsion to try to fix our loved one, at least for a while.

Jack and Eileen, whose only daughter became addicted to heroin after struggling with eating disorders for many years, believed that with proper treatment their daughter would give up drugs. They sent her to some of the most highly regarded therapeutic communities in the country and paid for psychiatric and residential treatment for several years.

As Jack expressed it, "Eileen and I both grew up in families where if something was wrong, you fixed it. If there was a problem, you took care of it. It was as simple as that. So when our daughter developed this problem, we said, 'Okay. Here's how we're going to handle it.' We got her into an excellent program. She completed it, and then we helped her get an apartment. She got a job, and we gave her a credit card for emergency use. We honestly believed everything was under control.

"Then we started getting these enormous credit card bills, and we finally told her we were closing the account. Then she called and told us she had relapsed, so we got her into another treatment program. To make a long story short, we spent a lot of money on different programs over three or four years. A lot of money. We were desperate. We were afraid she was going to die, and we finally had to face the fact that yes, she might die. This thing was bigger than anything we'd ever faced before. But we kept trying."

Hope and her husband took out a second mortgage on their house to pay for their daughter's first rehab treatment because they believed she deserved "the best." Their daughter relapsed shortly after completing the program. Then Hope started taking her daughter to state-funded treatment centers. She said, "If she didn't like a place, she'd leave, and I'd say, 'That's okay. You deserve something better.' I'd even look over places and turn my nose up at some if I thought they weren't good enough for my daughter. I must have taken her to every detox and rehab center in the state."

Hope also found what she thought was the ideal job for her daughter. "It was with a religious organization, and I figured being around all these church people would have a positive influence on her," Hope recalled. "She got fired for stealing five hundred dollars from them."

Audrey made it her business to call her son's counselor on a regular basis to find out how he was doing and to check up on what medications were being prescribed. "I thought the counselor and I were partners in this since we both wanted my son to get clean. We could kind of work together, you know? At first he was polite, but after a while he told me I should get my own counselor and stay out of my son's business. He finally stopped taking my calls," Audrey said, cringing at the memory. That didn't stop her from trying another approach. "I got so worried about my son I started calling the police and telling them when he was going out. 'He's gonna have drugs on him,' I'd say. I thought if he went to jail, he'd get clean. They'd tell me there wasn't much they could do about it."

Andy, married less than a year when his wife developed an addiction to painkillers, decided that the best way to solve the problem was to put her on a strict budget. He said, "I made her give me her paycheck every week. I gave her fifty dollars for lunch and spending money on Mondays, and it had to last. I put the credit cards and checking account in my name. I followed her to the gas station and paid for her gas. I bought the groceries. I didn't see how she could possibly afford to keep buying pills. But she managed. I think she was shoplifting, although she never admitted it."

Deb promised her addicted boyfriend that she'd marry him only after he'd been clean for at least a year. She settled for six months. Her hope that his heroin addiction was cured soon gave way to despair as he resumed his old pattern of sobriety and relapse. "It's like having your very own five-year-old child," she said, "and you have to watch out for him or something may happen, like the house may burn down or he may get into a car accident."

Celeste thought that reasoning would be the best way to persuade her son to get the help he needed for his addiction. "We'd have these long conversations about what addiction was doing to his life," she recalled, "and I'd feel like I'd really gotten through to him. I'd explain how addicts can't do it alone. They need to be in some kind of program to get better. I'd point out how drugs were ruining his life and how he had all these good qualities that were just being destroyed. He'd agree and seemed sincere. But after I left he probably went and shot up again. I don't know. We had these conversations over and over, and his problems just got worse and worse."

In their efforts to control the addict, many families become amateur detectives. They listen in on phone conversations and check out every unfamiliar number on their phone bill. They open their loved one's mail and pore over bills and financial statements. They check the mileage on the car, examine the person's clothing, count medications, go through his or her personal belongings with a fine-tooth comb, and engage in cat-and-mouse conversations aimed at uncovering some recent falsehood. "So, what time did you leave work today?" they might ask when they know their loved one took three hours to make the half-hour trip home. "How was the AA meeting?" they may inquire when they know that the addict did not attend the meeting.

Others prefer a more direct assault. "Where are you going and what time will you be back?" they ask. "Where have you been?" "Why are your eyes so red?" "Why are you wearing long sleeves?" "You look tired. What have you been doing?"

Whatever methods families choose to try to control the addict—and most of us try them all at one time or another— their efforts rarely produce the positive results they so desperately seek. Instead, the more consumed they are by their loved one's addiction, the more their own mental, emotional, and physical health is likely to suffer.

Toxic Shame

Addiction carries a stigma. Although attitudes are slowly changing as more families are impacted by the disease, the old stigma is still there. Part of it stems from the unfounded belief that addiction is a choice, or at the very least a sign of poor character. The regrettable behaviors that are characteristic of addiction perpetuate the stigma, which in turn intensifies the shame that most addicts feel. During his many years of homelessness, Brian remembers sleeping under trees and behind bushes and washing himself with Clorox wipes stolen from CVS. He felt he deserved the looks of disgust he often received from strangers. "I smelled disgusting and looked disgusting," he said, still struggling after three years of sobriety to let go of his shame.

But addicts aren't the only ones affected by shame. Many family members experience it too. When an addicted loved one causes a scene in public, gets fired or evicted, gets arrested, causes an accident, or in other ways brings unfavorable attention to the family, shame is often an instinctive reaction. We feel "less than" other families who seem untouched by such painful, dangerous, or embarrassing behaviors. And when friends and neighbors talk about a loved one's latest successes—a graduation, a promotion, a happy marriage or new house or great job—we compare them to our loved one's situation and feel the shame of not measuring up.

I remember skipping the wedding of a dear friend's daughter because I was afraid that someone in that celebratory crowd would ask about my own daughter, who, I was too ashamed to admit, was in jail. I hid at home, alone and miserable with a sense of failure and inadequacy. For in my singular focus on saving my daughter, her problems had become my problems. Her shame had become my shame.

I was convinced that everything she was going through was my fault. I replayed the many mistakes I'd made through the years over and over again in my head, certain that if I had been a better mother she never would have turned to drugs. I was unmoved by the familiar Al-Anon saying "You didn't cause it. You can't control it. You can't cure it." Maybe it applied to others, I thought, but not to me. I had failed my daughter. Worse, my personal shortcomings had propelled her into a life of self-destruction. Like my daughter, I was consumed by shame, and the only way to fix it was to fix her.

Without realizing it, I got stuck in an unhealthy pattern in which my shame made me vulnerable to constant lies and manipulation. I became a convenient scapegoat for her problems, creating a toxic dynamic of shame and blame in which her addiction flourished and my misery increased.

It would take years for me to fully grasp the destructive power of shame. For shame not only robs us of our sense of worth. It makes us believe that we're undeserving of happiness and undermines our ability to make the changes that are necessary to create a better life. The psychiatrist Carl Jung said it best: "Shame is a soul-eating emotion."

Unfortunately, shame and addiction seem to go hand in hand. For both addicts and the people who love them, one of the primary benefits of recovery is learning to heal the distorted thinking that leads to shame.

Sickened by Addiction

Sick at heart is the way most of us feel when faced with the addiction of someone we love. The phrase captures the suffering that family members endure and hints at addiction's subtle, pernicious effects on the overall health of everyone concerned.

Families undergo enormous prolonged stress when a loved one is addicted. They experience near-constant worry about immediate concerns: "Will the rent be paid?" "Has he let the car insurance lapse?" "Is she going to lose this job too?" "Is he going to cause an accident?" Crushing fears about the future abound as well: "Is she going to turn to prostitution?" "Is he going to end up on the streets?" "Are they going to send her to jail?" "Is he going to die?"

On top of their worry and fear, families experience the confusion that comes from repeatedly being lied to, the anxiety of never knowing what the next crisis will be, the frustration of doing everything within their power to help someone who refuses to be helped, the sorrow of watching a loved one slip away, and the disappointment of having their hopes raised only to be dashed yet another time.

It's no wonder that so many families of addicts suffer at least some of the ill effects of stress, which can include headaches, backaches, bowel problems, ulcers, high blood pressure, and heart disease, as well as insomnia, fatigue, appetite disorders, loss of sexual desire, exhaustion, and depression.

"I was out of my mind," Celeste recalled. "I couldn't sleep, and I was exhausted all the time. I'd go to the store for bananas and come home with broccoli. I'd be driving down a road and forget where I was going. I'd take an order from a customer and forget what they said before I hung up the phone. People must have thought I was nuts."

Other family members say such things as "I didn't go out for two years after I found out about my daughter's addiction." "I started taking antidepressants because all I did was cry." "Every day I'd go through the motions, you know, go to work, act like everything was all right, go home. But he was always there in my head." "I forgot how to have fun." "I walked around feeling like I'd been kicked in the gut. I never smiled."

Dealing with addiction can drain all the joy out of life, leading concerned family members to exist in a perpetual state of anxious exhaustion. The collateral damage of addiction doesn't stop there. Marriages can become strained as parents disagree about the best course of action. Children and spouses can feel abandoned as a family member showers unwavering attention on the addict and neglects everyone else.

"It seems like you have to be an alcoholic to get any attention in this family," a sibling may complain. "I don't have a wife anymore. All she thinks about is our son," a husband may say. Siblings or others close to the situation may see (with perfect clarity) that the addict is being rewarded for bad behavior when the family pays the car insurance bill or gives the addict yet another "loan" or finds the addict yet another job, apartment, counselor, or lawyer.

Under such unhappy circumstances, resentment and anger can build. One woman recalled that one of her sons beat up his addicted brother on more than one occasion, trying to "knock some sense into him." One father routinely berated his middle-aged alcoholic son with such comments as "You're a bum! You're disgusting. Look at what you've become. You're scum!"

Even those who have been the most patient with the addict, the most forgiving and loving and uncomplaining, may sometimes find themselves filled with rage. It is hardly surprising. Healthy love can flourish only within an environment of mutual respect and consideration, qualities that are in short supply in most addicts. Instead, addicts repeatedly hurt and disappoint the very people who care the most about them, and anger is a natural result.

One mother confessed that she was shocked to find herself screeching angrily at her heroin-addicted son one day. "I stopped by his house to see how he was doing, and for some reason I just snapped," she said. "The place was a pigsty, and he looked like a zombie. I lost it. I said, 'You're not even human anymore. You don't have any feelings, no emotions. You don't take pleasure in anything that's real. You don't care if the sun comes up or if it never comes up. You're nothing but a parasite, a hollow-eyed junkie. You disgust me!'"

One father admitted that he sometimes fantasized about hiring someone to beat some sense into his alcoholic son.

Some family members admit to harboring a secret wish that the addict would die. "At least I could mourn him and get on with my life," they may reason. "She's not really living anyway. God might as well take her so I can stop worrying," they may say. "Don't I deserve a little peace of mind before I die?"

Such sentiments are indicative of the deep suffering that many families of addicts experience. A sense of hopelessness can arise when every conceivable effort to save the addict has failed. When families have given everything they have to give, and when the only result seems to be endless unhappiness, they may long for an escape no matter what the cost.

What such families tend to forget is that they do not have to wait until their loved one has found recovery before they can begin to enjoy life again. In fact, families can rediscover simple pleasures, find ways to experience peace of mind, and even begin to laugh again—*no matter what the addict is doing.*

The key is for families to begin their own journey of recovery. The journey includes learning healthier ways of interacting with their addicted loved one and embarking on a path of personal growth and healing. As long as addicts and family members are locked in the destructive cycle of addiction, there is actually little hope that things will get better. "If nothing changes, nothing changes," as they say in Twelve Step meetings.

Family members who choose to break the unhealthy cycle *can* have a positive influence on their addicted loved one. More importantly, they can find peace of mind and reaffirm the value of their own lives. We'll examine some strategies for doing just that in chapter 7. But first we'll look at the process of change and its implications for our addicted loved ones.

SIX

The Process of Change

"The world as we have created it is a process
of our thinking. It cannot be changed
without changing our thinking."
—ALBERT EINSTEIN

A FRIEND OF MINE has been trying to quit smoking for years. She's tried everything she could think of: patches, gum, hypnosis, support groups, and therapy. She even taped some lurid pictures of smokers' lungs around her house, convinced that the glaring ugliness of the images would deter her from smoking. But her smoke-free lifestyle has never taken hold, and in a matter of weeks or months (once it was almost two years), she finds herself lighting up again. "I've seen the literature. I know the statistics," she'll say. "I'm killing myself, and I feel like a social pariah, hunching in doorways during my breaks at work. What will it take to make me stop?"

What indeed? My friend is facing the challenge of making a personal change, a challenge that addicts and their families know all too well. If changing our habits, attitudes, or desires were simply a matter of identifying a problem and deciding to fix it, then there would be little need for the self-help movement, psychoanalysis, or addiction treatment programs—or books like this! But the reality is that making any significant personal change is a daunting task. Add to that the psychological and physiological power of psychoactive substances, and the enormity of overcoming addiction becomes apparent.

It is, perhaps, the sheer magnitude of the challenges faced by addicts and their families that has led us to think of addiction treatment in terms of "recovery" rather than simply "change." *Change* connotes altering certain habits, perhaps replacing one pattern of behavior with another. On the other hand, recovery suggests something deeper and more profound—an inner transformation that broadens an individual's psychological and spiritual sensibilities.

A speaker I heard at an AA meeting alluded to this fundamental difference when he told the audience, "The man I was will always drink." He had become a new person, he suggested, with a new outlook on life and a different understanding of his world. It was this personal revolution that enabled him to remain sober. When those in the addiction community speak of "white-knuckling it" or say someone is a "dry drunk," they are referring to abstaining from drinking or taking drugs without achieving the self-awareness and personal growth that come with recovery in its fullest sense. Certainly, it is possible for some individuals to become abstinent without achieving recovery, and abstinence is in itself a monumental victory. But for many, the process of overcoming addiction requires the willingness to embrace a significant change in attitudes and perceptions.

Individuals who are "in recovery" are not just the same people with different habits. They are people who have experienced an inner enlightenment, people whose new choices and behaviors spring naturally from a transformed inner self. It's a lofty concept with roots in spiritual traditions that speak to the power of human beings to reinvent themselves and begin anew.

"This is all well and good," you may be thinking, "but it's the addict who needs recovery, not the family. After all, it's the addict who has the problem." This is superficially true, but as we saw in the previous chapter, many families eventually join their addicted loved one in a maze of denial, obsession, and unhealthy thoughts and behaviors. And although there are differences between an addict's and a family's search for recovery, there are distinct similarities.

For addicts, recovery implies a healing process that includes stopping the use of alcohol or other drugs, replacing harmful habits with healthful habits, building a secure sense of self, and developing a connection with something greater than themselves. Similarly, for families, recovery usually means healing the obsessive-compulsive fixation on the addict, replacing negative behaviors with positive ones, reaffirming their own self-identity, and nurturing a path toward spiritual growth.

Recovery for anyone is seldom an easy or straightforward process. In fact, it's likely to be complex, messy, and sometimes painful. To better understand how the process works, consider the following fundamental principles of how people change.

Prochaska's Model of How People Change

Most of us make large or small changes regularly throughout our lives. We get married or divorced, buy a new house, go back to school, find a different job, change our hair color, cancel a magazine subscription, take up a new hobby, go on a diet, redecorate the living room, and so on. Change is so natural, so inevitable, that we seldom stop to think about the process. However, sociologists and psychologists have given the matter some attention and have constructed a general blueprint of how people change.

The best-known model of change was proposed by James Prochaska, PhD, and his co-authors in *Changing for Good*. Prochaska became interested in how people break self-destructive

habits partly because of his own father's struggle with alcoholism. According to Prochaska, regardless of whether people are
attempting to make large or small changes, they all go through
the same six stages of change.

The first stage is called *precontemplation*. This stage is characterized by lack of awareness. Some people in this stage may
have an inkling that there's a problem, but they are not even
considering doing something about it. Others have no idea
that there's anything wrong. Even when problems are causing
difficulties in their lives, people in this stage are resistant to
the concept of change. Precontemplation can be summed up
by the words of eighteenth-century social commentator G. K.
Chesterton: "It isn't that they can't see the solution. It is that
they can't see the problem."

The second stage is *contemplation*. This stage is one of growing awareness. Individuals begin to see that there are problems
or that certain changes would be beneficial. Sometimes, but not
always, a confrontation or a crisis brings about this growing
awareness. Those in this stage are beginning to think about the
problem, but are not yet ready to do anything about it.

The third stage is *preparation*. People rarely make immediate changes. Rather, they take their time thinking about the
problem and evaluating their options. During the preparation
stage of change, individuals start making inquiries, consider
possible courses of action, and decide what steps they will take
to make a change.

The fourth stage is *action*. In this stage, individuals are
taking steps to alter their behavior. Whether small and tentative or large and bold, the actions taken during this stage are
intended to move individuals closer to the successful resolution of the problem. For example, people in this stage may have
enrolled in a class, bought a treadmill, entered rehab, or made
an appointment with a credit counselor. The key is that they

have engaged in some tangible act to address the problem and effect change.

The fifth stage is *maintenance*. This stage gets to the crux of the matter. Almost anyone can give up chocolate or begin an exercise program or turn off the television—once! It's the *permanent* establishment of a new pattern, a new habit, a new way of looking at things that's hard to accomplish. Ask anyone who's ever broken a New Year's resolution, which probably includes anyone who's ever made one. Because this stage is almost always the most difficult, relapses to earlier stages—even to the precontemplation stage—are common. That's okay. In Prochaska's view, progress is seldom linear. That is, people rarely set out on a course of change and proceed directly to their goal. Rather, they experience change as a spiral, where they inch forward, then fall backward. Move up, then down. The good news is that even as they relapse to earlier stages, they absorb lessons learned along the way. They are not completely unchanged, even though those changes may not be visible to others—or to themselves.

The sixth and final stage is *termination*. This stage is reached when the problem no longer exists, when the temptation to relapse is no longer present. Some psychologists doubt that this stage is ever fully experienced, noting, for example, that smokers who have been clean for twenty-five years or more may experience an occasional craving, even relapse. Nevertheless, those who have reached this stage have successfully incorporated change into their lives, making new habits, thoughts, or attitudes (often all three) integral parts of who they are.

The value of the stages of change model is that it helps us to recognize that change is a process with a predictable pattern and that setbacks are an almost inevitable part of the process. It is unreasonable to expect that everything can get better all at once or to fear that one mistake or relapse will negate the progress that's been made. Setbacks come with the territory, and some people must move through the spiral of change many times before they are able to achieve and maintain their goals.

Although Prochaska's model proposes a useful blueprint for understanding the general process of change, the larger questions, perhaps, are the following: Why is it that some people can go merrily along in the same damaging or dead-end routine for months and even years before they finally admit that they have a problem? And why is it that even when they recognize that something is wrong, they still can be frozen in inaction for a long time before taking those first tentative steps toward change?

More to the point, what does it take for an addict to decide to change? The following stories offer some valuable insights.

The Addict's Road to Recovery

A twenty-two-year-old woman who had been addicted to heroin since the age of sixteen was living a life of utter destitution. After serving a six-month jail sentence, she began spending her nights in a "wet shelter" (a shelter that does not require its clients to be clean and sober), sharing space with other destitute people and an army of cockroaches. Turned out of the shelter at seven each morning, she spent her days shoplifting or turning tricks, getting drugs and getting high, and huddling in the public library for warmth. She had attended dozens of treatment facilities over the years and spent hundreds of hours with counselors. Nothing worked, and she seemed destined to be destroyed by addiction. However, one day everything changed.

"I remember lying in the shelter one morning, shivering and shivering because I was dope sick," she recalled. "One of the women who worked there asked if I wanted to go to a detox, and I said yes. I knew they'd give me something for the pain. She punched out and used her own time to drive me to a detox center, which was really nice of her. They were busy that day, and I had to sit in the waiting room for eight hours. I watched *Titanic* twice on their little TV. While I was sitting there, this thought came to me: 'All I have to do not to live like this anymore is stop using drugs.' It was so simple—but so powerful. For years people had been telling me basically the same thing. Yet I never got it before. But that moment was the start of my recovery. I haven't used a drug since, and I've been clean for three years."

Brian, who had endured countless degrading and dangerous situations during his many years of homelessness, described the start of his recovery more succinctly: "I got tired of listening to the couple in the front seat beating the shit out of each other," he said. He decided to move into a wet shelter, signed up for an outpatient treatment program that he walked to every day, and eventually found a job and permanent housing.

Why these particular moments for these particular people? There is no definitive answer to that question. Perhaps lessons learned during repeated journeys through the spiral of change finally came together for them. Perhaps they were at a stage of psychological readiness. Perhaps they had finally reached their "bottom."

The mystery of why people start to get better at any given moment will probably always remain just that: a mystery. Yet certain factors seem to contribute to the desire to change, no matter how long the process may take. One factor is the accumulation of knowledge. Each time we enter a higher stage in the process of change (going from contemplation to preparation, for example), our understanding of the problem may expand, and our self-awareness may grow. Even mistakes and relapses can lead to greater knowledge that one day translates into the awareness and motivation necessary to make sustainable changes.

Jane, a heroin addict who was on the streets and in and out of jail over an eight-year period, described her recovery experiences this way: "Little things happened to me over the years. I remember looking through the prison fence, watching cars go by, and saying to this woman, 'Ooh, look at that one. Look at that one! When I get out, I'm going to ride in a car like that, 'cause I love cars.' And she gave me a look with those dead eyes of hers—she was in for life and everyone who's doing life has dead eyes—and said, 'The only difference between you and me is you get to go out for a while and ride in those cars, but you always come back.' And I thought, 'She's right.'

"Another time, I was in jail over Christmastime, and I called my mother. I think she knew I was there, but she didn't write to me. And I asked if she would please send me pictures of my kids, and she did. I was so happy. And actually, I started going to church when I was in prison, and every time I went to church, I would bawl my eyes out. So I told these people my mother sent me pictures of my kids, and I got classified for prerelease. The church people said, 'See, God's working in your life.'

"When I got out, I went into a sober house. I had to go to meetings, and I would listen to people's stories, but inside nothing changed. I thought to myself, 'If I have to stay sober and go to these damn meetings, then I'm going to steal stuff and I'm going to look good.' I got a sponsor. I got my one month, two months, three months clean. At five months I don't know what happened, but I wanted to get high. I was crawling out of my skin. I couldn't stand it and had to get high. I was so mad that I couldn't just go out and buy a bag of heroin because you gotta buy the works [syringe, cooker, and so on], find out where to buy it. So I put these cans of Spam together, and I tried to inhale it. I used to inhale all kinds of stuff when I was a kid: deodorant, furniture polish, everything. So I'm trying to inhale this Spam, and I thought, 'What the hell am I doing?' I put it down. I think that's where my recovery started."

However, Jane returned to drugs and then to prison one last time before her recovery finally took hold. She recalled: "When I got out of prison, they sent me to this halfway house that was brand new. Some AA women had started it. I was the only resident, and they didn't even have a director yet. So they'd come over and talk to me and take me shopping because all I had was my prison clothes. When I finished my six months, the newspaper did a story about me, and all these politicians were there for the photographs. And the women asked me to stay on as house manager, and it just grew from there. I think I didn't want to let them down."

For Jane, the accumulation of experiences, many of them terrible, some of them glimmers of light, slowly built the foundation for recovery. Seven years later, Jane is still clean. She went back to school, bought a house, and works as a counselor for addicted women.

Another factor in the decision to change is the accumulation of suffering. One night, not long after my daughter came home to live with me, I remember calling a crisis hotline to ask what I could do to help my daughter get off drugs. "She's so miserable. I know she wants to stop," I said, fighting back tears.

The man on the other end, a recovering addict, was not impressed. "A lot of people want a lot of things," he said. "I want a million bucks. But am I willing to do what it takes to get it? No." He went on to explain that *wanting* recovery—that is, wishing that it would somehow magically happen—and making a commitment to *getting* recovery no matter what the cost are two very different things. And until my daughter reached that level of commitment, she would probably not get better.

"What will it take to get her there?" I asked.

His answer frightened me.

"A lot of pain."

She had already suffered a lot of pain—the loss of her high school sweetheart, the loss of all her possessions, jobs, apartments, friends, opportunities, and self-respect—but perhaps all that was not enough. Perhaps the rewards, the pleasure that the drugs delivered, outweighed the suffering she endured.

"An addict has to hit bottom before he wants to recover," the man on the phone continued. "And no one knows what his bottom is until he gets there."

The concept of hitting bottom is a staple of the recovery community. It implies a situation so unbearable that getting better becomes the only viable option. When we think of "bottoms," we envision homelessness, jail, and dire physical illness. But not all addicts reach such depths before seeking and finding recovery. As one therapist expressed it, "You can get off the elevator at any floor." Most therapists agree that a primary goal for those who are trying to help an addict should be to "raise the bottom," that is, to nudge the addict toward recovery before the addict's life is in total ruin.

Mark, a married alcoholic with two children, recalled his "bottom" this way: "I'd been drinking heavily for years, and it was doing terrible things to my wife and kids. They couldn't stand being around me. I'd walk into a room, and they'd leave. I was an embarrassment. I looked like hell. I stank. On the job I was messing up all the time, but the boss was a friend and he kept letting me slide. I started getting really sick, and finally my wife made a doctor's appointment for me. She could barely stand me by then, but she's a compassionate person. She knew I was suffering. The doctor told me I didn't have long to live if I kept drinking. That was it. Stop drinking or die young. I started going to AA, and I haven't had a drink since."

He added, "Everyone's bottom is different. I never lost my family, my home, or my job. I was lucky. Given the choice of life or death, I chose life."

Not everyone can identify the moment of decision to get clean so precisely. Not everyone finds recovery at the same pace or in the same way. But addicts who make the transition from being an active user to a recovering addict seem to follow similar steps along their journeys. These steps include becoming aware of the problems addiction is causing in their lives, experiencing deep unhappiness with their situation, deciding that they want to overcome their addiction, and finding meaningful support for their efforts to recover.

As one therapist who has worked with addicted clients for more than twenty-five years explained, "Most addicts want to get clean, even if they are not ready to admit it. I don't know anyone who likes waking up dope sick every day. I don't know anyone who says, 'When I was a kid, my goal was to sell my body on the street or to live in crack houses and go to jail.' They have a terrible disease, but most of them want to get better. The trick is to tap into that desire and help them build on it."

The therapist went on to say that three things affect how somebody changes: (1) the unique set of strengths, weaknesses, and resources, including personality and family, that the individual brings to the situation; (2) the skills and tools, including education and awareness, that the individual acquires through treatment and experience; and (3) the support of a healing relationship with somebody else, such as a therapist, minister, or sponsor (a mentor in a Twelve Step program such as Alcoholics Anonymous or Narcotics Anonymous), who can help the individual mobilize personal strengths.

The recovery experiences of Lia, a twenty-two-year-old addict and alcoholic who has been clean and sober for more than a year, illustrate the complex and often lengthy process of overcoming addiction: "When I was seventeen, my parents put me into rehab. When I came out, I knew I wasn't going to give up drinking. I wasn't going to give up drugs. I still wanted to use heroin once in a while. I still thought I could do it.

"I got arrested for selling acid and spent three months in jail, and all I could think about was when I get out, I'm going to get a real job, go to school, go to the gym. Yet the first thing I did when I got out was use. I didn't want to live that lifestyle, but the other part of me couldn't wait to get out and shoot heroin.

"I wanted a good life, but I wanted to be able to get high. That was my goal, to be able to control my use of substances so I could be happy and still use. That was my goal since I was thirteen, trying to find a substance I could do and still be able to maintain life—still be able to drink and have fun, still be able to get high on heroin, but not have consequences.

"I had a month left on my probation that I wanted to clear up, so my parole officer advised me to go into rehab. I was living in a shelter because my parents wouldn't let me live with them, and I was still shooting up. I hated myself for using. I wanted to get clean, but I thought I had to do it myself. No one could help me. I'm unique. I'm different. And I never thought I'd give up drinking.

"So I got into a rehab, planning to stay just a month. I wanted to get clean really, really bad, but I didn't think recovery [Twelve Step programs] was how I was going to do it. I thought there were choices: I could go into recovery, I could move, or I could change my life this way or that. I thought there were options. Now I know recovery was my only option. Now I know there was no way in hell I could've ever gotten clean if I hadn't gotten into recovery. And most people out there who are using can't get clean and sober [without recovery], and if they do, they're miserable.

"Anyway, in rehab they talked about a Higher Power. I didn't know what that meant. I mean, I love nature and sunsets—things I obviously didn't make. Something bigger than me made them. I didn't see what that had to do with my life. But someone suggested I pray. That night and the next morning I got on my knees. I don't even know what I said. I just jumped up and started laughing, like 'Whoa. I can't believe I just did that.' I did that a few times. I didn't know if I believed in God. I felt ridiculous.

"I remember when I was sitting in group one day having a craving, and I could see myself sitting on the toilet or sitting on the bathroom floor, 'cause that's where I used to get high a lot. Instead of seeing the high, I saw the empty house and myself feeling like shit after the ringer. And that's what I remembered. I thought, 'Oh my God, this worked; maybe there is a power bigger than myself.' This thing is so much bigger than me. I can't control it. I thought for so long I had willpower and could stop. Now I realize that whatever made me out there is higher than me. That's the only thing that can help me.

"I stayed in rehab the whole six months and went to meetings [Narcotics Anonymous or Alcoholics Anonymous] every day for a year. Now I work Monday through Friday from nine to six. I go to meetings four nights a week and twice on Sundays. I go out and speak at meetings on Thursdays. I go to college one night a week. I hang out with my friends on Saturdays. That's my day off. I go to concerts, and you know what? I found out I can have fun without drinking. I used to always dance with a drink in my hand.

"But I don't take anything for granted. I know I'll always have this disease, just like some people have cancer or an allergy to something. I have an allergy to substances. I just hope I'm still clean a year from now. I will be."

Although Lia's early treatment experiences were not immediately successful, it is likely that some of the knowledge she gained stayed with her. By the time she was psychologically ready to get better (although she still resisted the idea of recovery and total abstinence), she was fortunate to enter a rehabilitation center that provided the support she needed. There she experienced an inner transformation—in her case, she found a Higher Power—that sustained her through difficult moments. She continues to get support from her sponsor and other recovering addicts in her Twelve Step meetings.

Obstacles to Recovery

Anyone looking at the hardships that Lia (like most addicts) endured during her years of active addiction might be puzzled by the inner conflict she felt over giving up substances. After all, alcohol and other drugs had brought her to her knees. Wouldn't she welcome the opportunity to rid herself of them forever? Wouldn't she regard them as an enemy rather than a temptation?

In fact, most addicts experience deep conflict about giving up their drugs of choice. As we have seen, change is hard for everyone. In addition, substances of abuse actually alter brain function, diminishing the ability to make rational decisions. And addiction creates physical and psychological dependence that can't easily be overcome.

But the ambivalence over whether or not to fight addiction goes deeper than that. Giving up alcohol or other drugs has far-reaching implications for addicts. After all, no matter how much misery the addiction has created, it has also provided significant rewards: the pleasure of feeling high, the sense of kinship with others who are making the same choices, the release from pain and stress, and the escape from overwhelming difficulties. Fighting addiction means becoming willing to face problems, perhaps for the first time, without a chemical crutch.

It means becoming willing to accept the consequences of past mistakes and to assume adult responsibilities. It often means giving up certain acquaintances, a lifestyle, and a sense of identity. It means saying goodbye forever to familiar behaviors and replacing them with new and often awkward-feeling choices. It usually means enduring suffering, anxiety, and depression without the numbing effects of substances.

Because of these significant obstacles, for many addicts, the fear of getting clean is greater than the fear of destitution and death. Yet sooner or later, most addicts do make some attempt to overcome addiction. When they do, they face serious challenges. Foremost among these is the power of the drugs themselves.

A body that is accustomed to the presence of an addictive substance screams out for that substance when it is withheld. These cravings are both psychological and physiological in nature and, according to most addicts, they are unimaginably powerful.

In Lia's words, "Early recovery is the worst place to be. You're crazy. I didn't know if I was coming or going. One minute I'd think, 'I'm really going to do this,' and then I'd just want to get out of there [rehab]. I'd get a craving really bad, a head rush, like an electric shock through your whole body, and I'd really want it. I'd just really want to get high. I'd be sitting there, and all of a sudden, I'd just want it so bad. I still do now."

Another obstacle to recovery is the addict's own despair. Addicts feel a great deal of shame about themselves, remorse for the harm they have caused others, and hopelessness about their ability to fix past mistakes. I remember confronting my daughter when I discovered evidence of her using and making some scathing remark about how great she must feel. Crying, she said, "It doesn't make me feel good. I feel so weak when I do it. I hate myself."

An alcoholic said, "When I saw the look in my kids' eyes and saw what I was doing to them, I felt like a piece of shit. I drank to pass out."

A cocaine addict recalled, "When I thought about getting clean, I'd feel sick. I'd lost my house, my car, my job, my driver's license. I had a ton of bills. Everybody was after me. I couldn't face it."

Jane, who lost custody of her two children during her years of addiction, said, "When I was in prison, these girls would say, 'I'm never going to do drugs again. I'm never coming back here.' And I said, 'When I get out, I'm doing a bag of dope.' That's what I lived for, because I'd already given my kids up, and I accepted it. I couldn't fix the problem. How could I take these two small children back and tell them I was so sorry?"

As if confronting cravings, self-loathing, and enormous problems weren't enough, many addicts seeking recovery also struggle with some form of mental or emotional disorder. As we saw in chapter 3, a significant number of addicts have underlying emotional or psychiatric conditions. Individuals who are suffering from co-occurring disorders—including schizophrenia, bipolar disorder, anxiety, and major depressive disorder—face major hurdles when fighting addiction. For these individuals, addiction has become the only path to feeling "normal"—to escaping the fear, confusion, emptiness, boredom, and pain within. I will never forget the words of my own daughter, who had suffered from depression since early adolescence, as I drove her to her first detox. She huddled in the seat beside me, looked straight ahead, and said in a small, bleak voice, "I feel so empty inside." What would fill that gaping hole within if not drugs?

Finally, addicts who are contemplating sobriety often face the obstacle of not having the tools and support they need to succeed. Many people who become addicted lose (or never learned) important life skills. Because addiction stunts growth by preventing them from tackling life's problems as they come, they fail to develop the emotional, social, and practical skills that are necessary for sober living. Effective recovery programs address this challenge by helping addicts to learn about the disease, take responsibility for their own personal growth, and develop a strong support network. In recovery, addicts discover that challenges that seem overwhelming can be met successfully when tackled "One day at a time."

Although families cannot solve their loved one's addiction problems (addicts must accept full responsibility for their own recovery), they can often play a meaningful role in the addict's search for recovery. In the next chapters, we will see how families can promote their loved one's recovery and explore some helpful ways for families themselves to recover from the damaging impact of addiction.

SEVEN

Promoting the Addict's Recovery

"Start where you are. Use what
you have. Do what you can."
—Arthur Ashe

A CLICHÉ IN THE TREATMENT COMMUNITY is "Insanity is doing the same things over and over and expecting different results." The truth of this statement often becomes evident when we're trying to help an addicted loved one. In our desperation to bring about some positive change, most of us try the same things again and again—from nagging and scolding to threatening and pleading to fixing and problem-solving—only to be devastated anew with each relapse or rebuff from the addict.

To make matters worse, many families come to believe that they themselves can never be happy until their loved one "straightens up." They put their own lives on hold and become hostage to the addiction, in the process abdicating responsibility for their own well-being. As their loved one's compulsion to drink or use other drugs continues, their own compulsion to change and control the addict intensifies. Thus the addict and the family become locked in a self-defeating maze of well-worn paths that lead only to stress and unhappiness, never release.

Trying to help someone overcome addiction can be like walking through a minefield. At each step, our best efforts can blow up in front of us, seeming to do more harm than good. I remember many times when I approached my daughter with what I thought of as gentle hints or well-meaning suggestions, only to be met with the angry assertion that my constant interference was only making her addiction worse. It took a long time for me to accept the fact that she could be right. At the very least, I wasn't helping.

Trying to change somebody else is always a risky business. It is human nature to resist others' attempts to force us to change. We want to be responsible for our own choices and live our own lives, no matter how much of a mess we might be making of things. When other people tell us we need to change, they seem to be saying that there is something wrong with us. This is criticism, and it cuts deepest when we fear it is true.

The other reason our efforts to help an addict can seem so futile is that the power of human persuasion is no match for the overwhelming power of addiction. Imagine trying to force someone to give up smoking or overeating. It is simply not possible to assert our will over another person's psyche. The resolve to give up smoking, gambling, overspending, or any number of detrimental compulsive behaviors that we humans engage in, including misuse of alcohol or other drugs, can come only from the person who is engaging in those behaviors. Nothing allows us to get inside somebody else's brain and engineer the changes in feelings, attitudes, and perceptions that form the foundation of any successful recovery.

That said, families can be of enormous value in helping their addicted loved one to reach a state of readiness for recovery, in "raising the bottom" for their loved one, and in supporting their loved one through the recovery process. They can do this by becoming healthier themselves and by employing some well-established strategies for dealing with addiction. Keep in mind that there is no "cookie-cutter" approach that will "solve" the problem of addiction, no "one-size-fits-all" solution to this deviously complex disease. Instead, there are general principles that can help families sow seeds of recovery both for their loved one and for themselves. By choosing to seek recovery, families can begin to reaffirm the value of their own lives and—perhaps—light the way for their addicted loved one.

Strategies for Supporting Recovery

Addiction is a chronic, progressive disease that usually gets worse without some form of intervention and treatment. Although families cannot control or cure their loved one's disease—the impetus for that change must come from somewhere within the addicted individual—families can create a recovery-oriented base of support that promotes the addict's willingness to get help. Many families have found the following strategies to be helpful.

Get Educated

When my daughter was a sophomore in high school, her behavior changed in disturbing ways. She dropped out of activities that she used to enjoy, including dance and voice lessons; she began skipping classes and was chronically late for school; her grades plummeted; she began selling personal possessions; her personal habits became slovenly; and she began lying to me on a habitual basis.

I suspected depression and took her to at least four child psychologists during the next two years. She refused to open up to any of them, but they all told me more or less the same thing: that my daughter was a normal teenager with a good head on her shoulders who was going through a particularly rough version of typical teen rebellion. I had nothing to worry about. Time would solve the problem.

None of them suggested that she might have a drug problem, and I was too deep in my own denial to even consider the possibility. Unfortunately, I was a classic example of "It can't happen in my family" thinking. It was only years later, after she had cycled down into heroin addiction, that she revealed that she had taken LSD more than fifty times in high school and had been routinely stoned on pot. In retrospect, it was obvious that most of her disturbing behaviors were classic symptoms of addiction.

I tell this story not to chastise the counseling profession—although I do feel that those four psychologists failed me and my daughter—but to illustrate the point that despite the enormous amounts of money being spent on the nation's war on drugs, there remains a dangerous lack of knowledge about drugs and their effects, not just among families, but among mental health professionals as well.

Addiction is truly one of the great social and medical dilemmas of our time. When addiction enters a family system, familiar relationships, rules, and routines are shaken. Certain rock-solid beliefs may fly out the window. During the early, shocking days of acknowledging the addiction, most families flounder through an emotional quagmire. Eventually, they seek answers. This is an important first step.

Getting educated about addiction is essential if families are to have any realistic hope of helping their loved one. In this respect, addiction is no different from any other disease: the more you understand about its nature, effects, and treatment, the more adept you'll be at responding effectively to the disease. A list of helpful sources of information, including other books and fact-based websites, appears at the back of this book. You can also ask questions of professionals, especially counselors who specialize in addiction.

Twelve Step meetings are also an important source of information. Joining an Al-Anon, Nar-Anon, or other support group for families of addicts may be critical for maintaining your own sense of well-being while learning about the disease. Attending a few open Alcoholics Anonymous or Narcotics Anonymous meetings is another excellent way to deepen your understanding of addiction. People who speak at these meetings are almost always in recovery, and their stories are usually enlightening and inspiring. The bottom line is this: the more families know about addiction, the more able they are to offer effective support.

Be Supportive

Being supportive does not mean we allow others to take advantage of us. It does mean showing others that we care, offering encouragement, and treating them with respect. Being supportive also implies that we ourselves are healthy and stable enough to provide support to others.

Most addicts have a deep well of shame and self-doubt. They need someone to believe in them because they don't believe in themselves. It's important that they hear such words as "I love you," "I know you'll get better," and "I'm here to help." Even if such remarks appear to make absolutely no difference, most addicts, like most people, will store these positive messages for later use. A friend of mine recalled that years ago, when she was falling apart over a broken relationship, a friend said, "I know you'll get through this because you're so grounded." She told me, "Ever since then, anytime I've felt totally lost, I remember that I'll get through it because I'm a grounded person." Jane recalled that during her years of active addiction, she often remembered the words of a favorite uncle who had reassured her mother, "Don't worry about Jane. Jane's going to be all right." She said, "I lived on that. I still do."

As one therapist explained, "Caustic words are rejected. They bounce off the person. Words like 'I love you,' 'I care,' 'I believe in you' are stickier. In a sense, they stick to the addict's skin and later work their way inside when they can have a positive effect."

Of course, being supportive is difficult when you're feeling frustrated, angry, or outraged. Sometimes an addict's behavior can become so destructive that the family chooses to limit contact with the person or to ask him or her to move out of the family home. In these situations, families can still be supportive by expressing themselves in terms of wanting to help. They can say to someone whose addiction is creating havoc in the home, "You can't live with us right now because being here isn't helping you. We can't give you what you need." They can then suggest alternative living arrangements such as a residential program.

In the case of minor children, parents should seek guidance about how to proceed. The decision to ask a minor child to leave home is one that should be made only with professional guidance and only as a last resort. One counselor observed, "Parents who are advised to use 'tough love' sometimes think the best answer is to throw the kid out. These kids often end up getting into things they may never have gotten into if their parents had taken a different approach."

Even when families make the painful decision to distance themselves from their loved one, they can frame their decision in terms of care and support: "We love you. We believe in you. When you're ready to get help, we'll be here for you."

Don't Enable the Addiction
The distinction between helping and enabling can be confusing. *Enabling*, as the word is used in the treatment community, is any action that in any way makes it easier for someone to continue using. Some family members define it as doing for the addicts what they can and should be doing for themselves. For example, loaning an addicted person twenty dollars is a clear case of enabling. In this case, the loan will make it easier

to purchase drugs. Paying an addict's bills is enabling. Lying and covering up for the addict is enabling. Often it is easy to identify an enabling act, even though it is not always easy to prevent ourselves from doing it. At other times, enabling is not so easy to spot.

What, for example, are parents to do if their daughter has no food in her house because she has spent her money on drugs? Surely buying her groceries is not enabling. The question becomes even more complicated if there are grandchildren involved. How can the parents not pay the rent, buy the food, and pay the heating bill when innocent children might suffer? Is it enabling to rescue a sick and hurting person from living on the streets?

The sad truth is that anytime we do anything to prevent our addicted loved ones from fully experiencing the consequences of their actions, we are enabling. I was aware of this when I let my daughter continue living with me even after she broke my rule of not using drugs in my house. I was aware of this when I signed for her second and third car loans. I was aware of this when I put gas in her car so she could get to work.

These decisions were based on my evaluation of the situation and my own sense of what I could live with. She was working, she paid her bills, she was going to counseling and Twelve Step meetings, and she was (usually) respectful of me. Since she was making at least some effort to get better, I did not feel it was wrong to offer her help in these ways. I also felt I could not live with myself if I didn't at least know that she had a roof over her head at night. However, since my actions made her using easier, I was undoubtedly guilty of enabling.

Like me, most families struggle to define the line between helping and enabling. Sometimes families are forced to make painful decisions. To offer a helping hand to a family member in need is normal. Unfortunately, it is also normal for addicts to prey on family members who want to help. One way to sort through this thorny issue is to ask ourselves if our actions are supporting addiction or recovery. We won't always get it right, but we'll at least have some basis for our decision-making.

Detach with Love

Anyone who's ever attended a Twelve Step meeting knows that *detachment* looms large as a way to cope with an addicted loved one. "Detach with love," we're told, "if you want to preserve your sanity." Which is all well and good, I used to think, but what about my daughter? Don't I have a duty to try to help? Doesn't detachment seem a little bit *selfish*? A little bit like *giving up*?

It can definitely feel that way at first, especially if we've come to believe that our loved ones can't get clean without us. But here's the problem: the longer we're a passenger on the roller coaster of addiction, the less we're able to provide any meaningful help. When we're right there with them through those peaks and valleys, we can't step back, regain our balance, and offer the kind of clear-sighted support that might make a difference.

Detachment is neither unkind nor unloving. It's simply a recognition of the fact that we can't live our loved ones' lives for them. When we accept this fundamental truth, we begin to understand that detachment is actually good for our addicted loved ones.

For one thing, detachment allows us to let go of expectations that perpetuate shame. As we've seen, most addicts don't like themselves very much. On some level, they know they're messing up their lives, but they don't know how to stop. Their sense of shame grows deeper every time they see us look at them with disapproval or disappointment and every time we resort to nagging, scolding, crying, threatening, shaming, and other manipulative behaviors. Our obsessive watchfulness gives our loved ones one more reason to feel bad about themselves, and one more reason to use. Detaching from our expectations of them reduces our loved ones' shame, granting them the space to find their own way.

Detachment also gives addicts the opportunity to learn from the consequences of their own choices. It would be great if we could learn important life lessons simply by being warned about negative consequences. If that were the case, we'd all make fewer mistakes and have fewer regrets to look back on. Unfortunately, most of us have to learn through experience, which means facing the consequences of our choices. That includes addicts. To fully comprehend the negative effects that substances have on their lives, they have to suffer the consequences of their choices. When we detach from their problems, we allow them to do that.

Finally, detachment allows addicts to experience the satisfaction that comes from personal accomplishment, while depriving them of a convenient scapegoat when things go wrong. Sometimes, when we solve problems for our addicted loved ones, things turn out well. The trouble is, these are our accomplishments, not theirs. They don't get to experience the satisfaction and build the self-esteem that come from knowing they did it on their own. On the other hand, when our problem-solving goes wrong, our addicted loved ones can point the finger of blame at us: "This is your fault. You set this up and now look what happened." Even if it's our loved ones who turned a great opportunity into a disastrous mess, our involvement makes us the target of their anger and disappointment. Instead of looking at their own role in the outcome and learning from the experience, they look at us.

By detaching from our loved ones, we let go of trying to solve their problems, giving them the opportunity to learn from their own failures and successes.

Let Crises Happen

One of my favorite sayings from Al-Anon literature is "In nature there are no punishments or rewards. There are consequences." This statement takes the right or wrong out of a situation, removes labels, and offers the plain, objective observation that choices have consequences. In scientific jargon, for every action there is a reaction. This is an important lesson for addicted people to learn. They must learn it if they are to begin recovery.

Psychological maturity comes from facing the inevitable challenges of daily life. In a sense, life is a series of challenges and problems that must be addressed if we are to live healthy, productive lives. Each time we face a challenge, we have an opportunity to learn and grow. Even failures can teach valuable lessons that help us mature. But avoiding life's challenges stunts our growth and keeps us immature.

Addicts are avoidance pros. Instead of trying to deal with life and its inevitable pain and hardships, they escape through the use of mind-altering substances. When they're doing poorly in school, they use drugs. When they feel abandoned by their parents, they get drunk. When they lose a job, they get high. When they feel bored, they get stoned. When they feel angry at the world, they get blotto. Instead of facing an issue, perhaps asking for help and trying to find a solution, they disappear through their chemical escape hatch. This keeps them perpetually immature and unable to cope with life in any constructive way.

When families help addicts avoid the consequences of their actions—which might be losing a home or job, going hungry, going to jail—the families are depriving them of an opportunity to grow. Likewise, when families are able to step back and let events follow the natural course, they are giving their loved ones a chance to learn valuable lessons. The phrase *growing pains* comes to mind here, reminding us that human growth often involves some pain. By letting their loved ones feel the pain of addiction, families are leaving the door to recovery wide open.

Learn to De-escalate

It's hard to support recovery in a chaotic environment. Yet because addicts' emotions are so volatile and their thinking so muddled, any interaction with them can quickly deteriorate into an angry confrontation. When well-meaning family members suggest that the addict needs help, they are often met with resistance and hostility. That's because the addict feels threatened. Even when the destructive impact of addiction is painfully apparent, most addicts will cling to the addiction, often using predictable tactics: deny, deflect, and diminish. Here's an example:

> **Mom:** I'm concerned about you. I want to help you get help for your problem.
>
> **Son:** I don't have a problem. (Deny) What about you? You take antidepressants. You're a terrible mother. (Deflect) Anyway, I only take a couple of pills a day to relax. (Diminish)

Each of these responses is an attempt by the son to divert his mother's attention away from his addiction. Each opens the door to an argument in which accusations fly, defensiveness grows, and nothing positive gets accomplished. But there are de-escalation techniques that family members can use to defuse tensions and promote a more positive outcome.

1. **Keep your focus on your goal,** which in this case is to encourage the son to get treatment. Don't allow yourself to get sidetracked into other issues. When the addict wants to talk about your faults or his horrible childhood, either end the conversation or remind the addict that you want to help.

2. **Practice patience.** Remember that addiction is a disease that creates confused thinking. Outrageous statements and irrational ideas come with the territory. They're not worth arguing about. One woman told me that when she senses an argument is about to erupt, she pictures her husband as a bottle of beer. "I wouldn't talk to a bottle, so why would I talk to him when he's like that?" She's learned not to bring up difficult topics when he is under the influence.

3. **Keep your emotions in check.** Addiction triggers emotional extremes. These can best be dealt with in an atmosphere of calm rationality. When things heat up, it's sometimes a good idea to back away with a statement such as "Let's discuss this later."

4. **Avoid falling into the "drama triangle,"** a set of behaviors described and modeled in the 1960s by Dr. Stephen Karpman. In these scenarios, participants alternately play the role of victim, persecutor, and rescuer, and nothing gets resolved. For example:

> **Wife** (persecutor): Your drinking is ruining our marriage.
> **Husband** (victim): I know. I'm a terrible person. You must hate me.
> **Wife** (rescuer): Of course I don't hate you. You have so many wonderful qualities.
> **Husband** (persecutor): Well, I wouldn't have to drink if you weren't such a bitch.
> **Wife** (victim): I try not to nag. It's just that I get so worried.
> **Husband** (rescuer): You shouldn't worry so much. Things aren't that bad.

Wife (persecutor): You say that because you're always drunk.

Husband (victim): I've cut back, but nothing I do is good enough.

Conversations like these go 'round and 'round, with both players vying for the role of victim (who has suffered the most?). Anger grows, frustration mounts, and the goal of encouraging the addict to get help gets lost in the turmoil.

Learning to de-escalate can help minimize the chaos that usually comes with addiction. By remaining calm and clear-headed, family members can create a less stressful environment that may encourage the addict to accept treatment.

Don't Scold, Criticize, Shame, or Reject

Most addicted people feel a great deal of self-loathing. Often these negative feelings prolong their addiction. Sometimes families hope that if addicts feel bad enough about themselves, they will want to change. The opposite is usually true. As Lia explained it, "If somebody gives you tons of stuff, that's enabling. If someone just ditches you, that just makes you go out there and use."

I remember ranting at my daughter one night, saying something like, "What's the matter with you? Can't you see what you're doing to yourself? Can't you learn from your mistakes?" I later asked Mark, a recovering alcoholic, what he thought about such tactics. He said, "If someone said that to me, I'd think, 'I guess I can't learn from my mistakes. I guess I'm just stupid. I might as well go have a drink.'"

Making people feel bad about themselves is never an effective way to encourage them to change. Instead, it makes them discouraged and hostile. If families are seething with anger (which at times they may well be) or filled with frustration (which is almost inevitable), they need to process these emotions in a healthy venue so they don't do damage to themselves or to their addicted loved ones. Counseling can help. It's also helpful to remember a rule of thumb heard in Twelve Step meetings: "If you can't help an addict, at least don't hurt him."

Jane feels grateful for the way her mother handled her years of active addiction. "My mother was devastated. She drew the line and refused to rescue me. But she wasn't mean about it," she said. "She calmly told my kids it was drugs. 'Your mother is very sick, but maybe someday she'll find her way back,' she said to them. Her kindness helped a lot when I was finally ready to get better."

A subtle but not harmless form of criticism occurs when we consistently try to exert our control over our loved ones. When we tell them to call their counselor, inquire about a job, or get the oil changed in their car, we are saying we don't think they're bright or capable enough to consider these things themselves. They may well have proven to us that they won't do these things on their own, but nothing can be gained, and much can be lost, by assuming their responsibilities. When people do things because we told them to, we have deprived them of the satisfaction of solving a problem on their own and given them an opportunity to blame us for the outcome. Thus, controlling perpetuates the very immaturity that we would like our loved ones to overcome.

Often our attempts to control are disguised as encouragement, such as when we suggest that they could do so much more with their lives or look so much better if they dressed or wore their hair a certain way. When we tell others how they should live or act, we are telling them they are not good enough as they are.

A counselor pointed this out to me when I said of my daughter, before her addiction problems fully blossomed, "She has so much potential. She could do so much." The counselor said, "When you say that to her, she doesn't hear encouragement. She hears criticism of who she is now. She hears she's not good enough." Of course, I did want her to change the direction of her life, but my clumsy efforts to control her choices were actually doing more harm than good. I had yet to learn the difference between encouragement and criticism.

Be Consistent

Addicts live in a shifting world of lies, deception, and self-delusion. They are experts at twisting the truth and at convincing themselves (and often their families) of the validity of their misperceptions. Everyday reality can become ill-defined, even nonexistent, to clouded minds. Yet if addicts are to recover, they must learn to function within the common boundaries of society, to find their place in the world of every day. Families can help by creating an environment that is consistent, dependable, and grounded.

This can be hard to do when families themselves are floundering in the mire of addictive behaviors. Nothing has prepared most families for dealing with the irrational, often-bizarre world of addiction, and it is easy to get caught up in destructive patterns without even realizing it. Yet many families have found the following four tactics helpful for promoting normalcy and building consistency into their relationships with their addicted loved ones.

1. **Avoid setting unreasonable ultimatums and inappropriate consequences, especially for minor children.** Threatening to throw a child out for "taking one more drink" is an example of such behavior. Following through on this threat would be punitive and unhelpful, and failing to follow through would undermine the parent's authority. (Making idle threats is a bad strategy in any relationship.) Although families may

have to establish rules and consequences, they should do so in moments of clarity, not in anger. Professional guidance can be helpful in setting realistic guidelines that families can live with.

2. **"Say what you mean and mean what you say, but don't say it mean."** This advice, often heard in Twelve Step meetings, addresses the communication problems inherent in any relationship with an addicted person. Talking to an addict can feel like walking on eggshells.

To me, talking to my daughter felt more like tiptoeing through a minefield. I never knew what benign remark might set off a bout of tears, rage, panic, or stony silence. I hesitated to say, "Your bathroom is a mess," "Your clothes are all over the house," or "You burned holes in my blankets." I found it almost impossible to talk about my core concern: her addiction and recovery. Intimidated by her instability, I lived for long periods in an uneasy truce with her during which neither of us talked about what was on our minds. This state of affairs felt dishonest to me, and I worried that she thought she was keeping her drug use hidden from me or—worse—that I didn't really care about her.

Gradually, with the help of a counselor, I learned that I had a right to express my feelings regardless of what her reactions might be. I learned to make "I" statements, such as "I don't like it when you make a mess of my stuff" or "I'm concerned about you, and I'd like to know how things are going." I might say, "I worry when I don't hear from you" or "I won't sign for another loan for you. I told you that, and I meant it." I also learned to sort through the conflicting thoughts in my head by asking myself, "Do I want to say something because I think that doing so will change her, or do I want to say it because that's how I honestly feel?" By consciously examining my motives, I learned to reduce some of the chaos in our household.

When we speak honestly with no expectations about our loved one's response and no motive other than to express our feelings, we lay the foundation for open communication and set a tone of truthfulness, both important elements of anyone's recovery.

3. Remind yourself, "You don't have to go to every battle you're invited to." Another gem heard in Twelve Step meetings, this saying hints at the emotional upheaval wrought by addiction. Addicts give us lots of opportunities to get worked up. They break their promises, don't follow through on commitments, deceive and mislead us, and do their best to manipulate us into giving them what they want. If we react to everything they say or do, our lives will be permanent chaos. This type of reacting does nobody any good. We can create a saner, less fractious relationship with our loved ones by learning to avoid unnecessary conflicts.

One man recalled, "My daughter knew how to push my buttons. We were always at each other's throats until I figured out that I didn't have to react to everything she said or did. I could walk away. Sometimes I'd even get in my car and go for a drive rather than listen to her nonsense."

Evading troubling issues simply to avoid a confrontation or crisis isn't helpful. However, neither is it helpful or useful to react to every problem that presents itself. Learning to overlook the small things helps us find the emotional energy to deal rationally and consistently with the core issues that must be addressed.

4. Get honest about your own substance issues. Many counselors point out that when someone has an addiction problem, frequently other substance use may be going on within the family. One teenager exclaimed angrily to his parents during a therapy session, "Why are you busting my balls? The two of you smoke pot every night!" I struggled with this issue myself after my daughter came home. I often had a glass of beer or wine in the evening, yet I wanted her to be abstinent.

Did that mean I had to give up my small pleasures? Unfortunately, yes. That glass of beer was not more important than my being a model of abstinence for her. I began practicing what I was preaching.

Counselors advise that, in the grand scheme of things, it is helpful to establish a dry household while someone is in the early days of recovery. For the alcoholic in the family, seeing others drink can be a trigger. While recovering addicts and alcoholics must learn to be abstinent in a world in which alcohol and other substances are plentiful, establishing a dry household, even for a short time, can underscore our support for recovery. As is always the case, our message is stronger when our actions match our words.

Encourage the Addict to Get Treatment

Addiction is a complex disease of mind, body, and spirit. Although some individuals are able to overcome addiction entirely on their own, most require some form of assistance to guide and support their recovery efforts.

The question of how much effort families should put into getting their loved one into treatment is hard to answer. After all, we want to detach from their problems. And responsibility for recovery rests squarely on the shoulders of the addict. As one detox center employee caustically pointed out to me, "Your daughter didn't need your help to find drugs. She doesn't need your help to find recovery." Yet I wanted her to get help, and when she seemed receptive to my offer, I contacted a treatment program and took her to an intake meeting. (This did not turn out to be the quick fix that I was hoping for, but it was the first exposure to the treatment community for both of us.)

Families cannot force their loved one to get help, except in the case of minor children. But they can provide information, such as phone numbers of social service agencies or lists of AA or NA meetings. They can say such things as "I'm concerned. I know there are people who can help you" and back up their words with an offer to help their loved one make the appropriate connections. Often, addicts are most receptive to offers of help when they are at a low point, such as when they're feeling vulnerable, remorseful, or depressed. It is almost always a waste of time to try to convince people who are under the influence of alcohol or other drugs that they need help. But when the high has worn off, when the addict is again enduring the bleak aftermath of intoxication, family members have an opportunity to encourage their loved one to get help and to propose some treatment options. Among those options are Twelve Step programs, individual counseling, and inpatient or outpatient care in a specialized facility.

For many addicted individuals, Twelve Step programs become the backbone of recovery. The meetings provide a wonderful source of support, encouragement, and hope and are absolutely free and available almost everywhere in the world. Alcohol and other drug users can attend whatever meetings are most comfortable for them, whether Alcoholics Anonymous, Narcotics Anonymous, or other Twelve Step programs. The principles and the meeting procedures are identical. Furthermore, although the programs are based on spiritual principles of humility and self-knowledge, they are not religious. Members are free to believe whatever they wish. Also worth noting is that addicts need not be drug- or alcohol-free to attend meetings. They need only be willing to listen or have a desire to stop using.

Twelve Step programs are truly a gift to the world, offering the opportunity to share deep personal feelings on a level that is rarely experienced elsewhere in our society. These meetings can be invaluable in helping addicts and family members build a support network and acquire the tools they need to achieve and sustain recovery. But Twelve Step programs are not for everyone.

One popular alternative to Twelve Step programs is SMART Recovery, which developed out of the Rational Recovery movement of the 1980s. Meetings, led by trained facilitators, are free and emphasize self-empowerment and self-reliance. The focus is on building and maintaining motivation; coping with urges; managing thoughts, feelings, and behaviors; and living a balanced life. The four-point program has earned recognition from many entities, including the American Academy of Family Physicians and the National Institute on Drug Abuse (NIDA).

Professional treatment programs offer a more structured approach. NIDA guidelines state that the goal of effective programs is to help addicts to "stop using drugs, stay drug free, and be productive in the family, at work, and in society." In addition, programs should "address all of the patient's needs, not just his or her drug use" through a combination of behavioral counseling, medication, "evaluation for co-occurring mental health issues," and "long-term follow-up to prevent relapse."

It's important to note that even the "best" treatment programs cannot force someone to give up alcohol and other drugs, and that even poorly staffed and underfunded programs can be effective. The key ingredient is readiness—how committed the addict is to recovery. Highly rated programs may be more successful at fostering readiness and commitment, but almost any program can be helpful when the addict is ready to get better.

Broadly speaking, treatment is available in three different settings: inpatient, outpatient, and extended care. Many inpatient facilities have medical units equipped to safely handle detoxification, the initial phase of care in which addictive chemicals are cleansed from the body. Inpatient treatment generally lasts from seven to twenty-eight days, although some facilities offer programs lasting six months or longer. During treatment, patients are completely immersed in recovery. They learn about the physical and psychological impact of addiction and begin to develop tools for maintaining abstinence.

Some outpatient programs are designed primarily to educate participants about the effects of alcohol and other drugs, while intensive outpatient programs are similar in scope to inpatient treatment. They combine education about the disease of addiction with group counseling and individual therapy. They focus on helping patients develop the skills and motivation necessary for sustaining sobriety. Most intensive outpatient programs require patients to attend sessions several hours a day, five days a week over a period of a month or more.

Extended programs—sometimes up to a year or more—are post-treatment facilities designed to help patients re-enter society while living in a highly supportive environment. Halfway houses, a common type of extended care program, encourage residents to work, develop social networks, and build day-to-day living skills. Most have on-site Twelve Step meetings as well as house managers who monitor the progress of residents' recovery.

Another option has been shown to be effective in the treatment of opioid addiction: medication-assisted treatment. Methadone, a synthetic opioid, has been used for more than fifty years as long-term replacement therapy for opioid dependence. Newer medications including buprenorphine and naltrexone have been proven effective in blocking the high produced by opioid use, decreasing opioid cravings, and reducing the risky behaviors associated with HIV infection and criminal activity.

Medically assisted treatment has been stigmatized by some in the recovery community who view it as a deviation from the "abstinence-only" model. These same people would not frown on someone using antidepressants, blood thinners, diabetes medication, or other medicines needed to combat chronic conditions. The reality is that brain function is damaged by addiction. Medications that help restore normal functioning have been lifesavers for many recovering addicts, allowing them to live healthy, productive lives. There is no reason to add another layer of stigma to an already stigmatized disease.

No matter what kind of treatment an addict receives, recovery is usually a long-term process. Relapse is common, and treatment may not bring about desired changes the first, second, or even third time around. Nevertheless, each attempt is an important step toward recovery, and families should not be discouraged from urging their loved one to get help when the time seems right to do so.

Conducting an Intervention

Many addicted individuals are resistant to the idea of getting help. They insist they are okay, that they can quit anytime, or that the family is making a big deal out of nothing. Denial is the nature of the disease of addiction. Although an addicted person's own experiences may eventually lead him or her to seek help, sometimes interventions are helpful in jump-starting the process.

Broadly speaking, interventions are acts that interrupt the progression of addiction, sometimes marking a turning point toward recovery. Interventions can be disruptive events, such as getting arrested for driving while intoxicated, going to jail, or getting fired from a job. Involuntary commitment to a treatment facility is another type of disruptive intervention, commonly referred to as being "sectioned." In this case, families turn to the court system to force their loved one into treatment. They are often desperate when they make this difficult decision (as I was when I sectioned my daughter, who seemed on the verge of dying), but the long-term value of sectioning is debatable. On one hand, the addict is humiliated by being apprehended by police, handcuffed, and taken into court like a criminal. Anger and resentment are the natural reactions. On the other hand, being in treatment for even a short time may clear the addict's thinking and spur recovery. It may even save the addict's life. As one mother explained: "My daughter overdosed twice in twenty-four hours. Getting her committed was the only way I could keep her alive."

Addicted individuals may not get better after such experiences—they may even get worse—but at the very least, these types of events disrupt the pattern of addictive behavior, alert addicts to the consequences of their use, and give them a chance to find recovery when they're ready.

Less dramatic informal interventions can also be of value. A recovering alcoholic remembered a friend saying, "I have observed that your drinking is causing problems." Although he heard little else that she had to say, that remark stayed with him. It raised his level of awareness, and he eventually sought recovery. Another man stopped drinking after ash from his cigarette fell and burned a hole in a $150 pair of pants. "I was used to taking from six to twelve drinks a day, but I never touched another drop after that happened," he recalled.

Simply changing a routine can also interrupt a pattern of substance use. A counselor related the story of how some boys in a group home would pool their weekly allowance and buy large quantities of pot and alcohol on the weekend. Several ended up in the hospital with alcohol poisoning. Since the allowance was state mandated, counselors could not withhold it. Instead, they moved allowance time from Friday afternoons to Monday mornings. By the time weekends came, most of the money had been spent on candy and other incidentals. "By disrupting the pattern, reorganizing it, we got a different outcome," the counselor said. "We never had the problem with substances again." He added that the home also provided counseling and education as part of a larger plan of intervention.

Small interventions happen whenever something occurs that disrupts the usual pattern of addictive thoughts and behaviors. In a sense, families are doing small interventions when they stop engaging in unhealthy interactions such as nagging, arguing with, or enabling their addicted loved one, and when they start practicing healthier ways of dealing with issues.

Larger, planned interventions are carefully orchestrated events designed to bring about abstinence and recovery. Although they can be quite effective, they can also be counterproductive if the addicted individual feels ridiculed, humiliated, chastised, or rejected. Planned interventions are best done with assistance from an addiction treatment professional.

In general, formal interventions consist of several steps. First, an organizer recruits concerned friends and family members to participate in the event. The organizer or professional facilitator also makes arrangements with a treatment facility so the addicted individual can go directly from the intervention into treatment.

Second, each participant writes a letter that expresses affection, concern, and clear, specific observations about the negative impact of substances on the individual's life. It is important that concrete examples of negative behaviors be given. Avoid such general, accusatory phrases as "You've become insensitive," "You've let yourself go," or "You've gained a lot of weight."

Third, because emotions will usually run high during an intervention, participants read their letters out loud during a rehearsal. This helps them maintain a tone of objectivity during the actual event.

Fourth, participants gather at a meeting place, taking the target of the intervention by surprise and at a time when the individual is not likely to be under the influence of alcohol or other drugs.

Fifth, with the guidance of a professional facilitator, participants read their letters, taking care to maintain a tone of love and concern.

Finally, the addicted individual is informed that treatment has been arranged and is urged to enter the treatment facility. These six steps are a much-abbreviated version of a formal intervention. Calling a professional interventionist or seeking guidance from a reliable source can add valuable information. Staging such an event is almost always fraught with anxiety, but interventions are really an opportunity for family members to express their love and concern for their addicted loved one.

Peter was in his early thirties when he decided to arrange a formal intervention for his father. He explained, "Dad's drinking had been a problem for years. My mother and he had the classic codependent relationship where he would drink and she would nag. I was after him all the time too. It was almost like a game in that he'd try to outsmart us by sneaking drinks when he thought we wouldn't notice. After [Mom] died, he got worse. He'd be drinking by nine in the morning, and he got all bloated and the blood vessels in his face began to break. He'd been very successful in his career, but he began having a lot of problems at work. My worry about him was also causing a lot of problems in my own life. I decided to organize an intervention as a last resort. I thought of it as my final effort to help him. If it didn't work and he insisted on drinking himself to death, I would at least know I'd tried everything I could."

Peter called in a professional to help. He recalled the following from the intervention: "Dad sat there smoking a cigarette, looking at each person in turn without a word or flicker of expression. After we'd all read our letters, he said, 'Where do I go?' We had arranged for a stay in a residential facility, and after that he went into a day program. He's been sober ever since and is doing consulting work and traveling a bit. Looking back, my impression of him during the intervention was of a little kid who finally realizes that all these people love him. He finally got the attention he'd always wanted."

Lynn is a recovering alcoholic who was on the receiving end of an intervention organized without professional assistance. She recalled, "I was an active alcoholic for about four years. Through this period, I alienated many, many people. I was totally obnoxious when I was drunk. I was also an impossible mother, and my son and I had what surely must have been one of the worst relationships in the history of parenthood. Fortunately for me, I also had many friends who responded with love rather than censure. They did an intervention on me, and it was a dreadful experience. I was horrified. I resented everyone terribly at the same time that I recognized their love and concern."

She continued, "The intervention was not what turned the tide. Instead, it was one friend who was there. He knew that the intervention hadn't had the effect that they all had hoped for, so he followed up. He arrived at my door one morning and walked me down to an outpatient alcohol-abatement service. It ran every weekday from 4:00 to 9:00 p.m. for five weeks. I signed up, and that was what did the trick. Oddly enough, once my head was pointed in that direction, quitting drinking was easy, and the behaviors fell away like so much rain. I think interventions can be helpful, but I believe follow-up is necessary."

Whether small or large, formal or informal, interventions can be effective tools for helping addicted individuals see their situation in a new light. Even if an intervention is not immediately successful, it can plant seeds of awareness that later blossom into a desire for recovery.

As we have seen, there are many strategies and behavioral skills that can help us promote our loved ones' recovery. But family members also suffer as a result of addiction, and the disease takes a terrible toll on our physical, mental, and emotional health. In the next chapter, we'll look at some effective ways to nurture our own recovery.

EIGHT

Promoting the Family's Recovery

"We can always begin again."
—JACK KORNFIELD

MANY FAMILIES FEEL GUILTY about seeking recovery for themselves. They ask, "How can we try to live a more serene life when our loved one is suffering so terribly?" or "What right do we have to happiness when this person we love is falling apart?" It can be hard to imagine that the despair can be lifted before the addiction has been overcome. It's tempting to believe that normal life must come to a stop until the addiction has been addressed.

In reality, the exact opposite is often true. In my experience, and in the experience of many people I have talked with, the family's recovery often precedes the recovery of the addicted individual. That's probably because families in recovery learn to avoid destructive patterns that may actually prolong addiction. They become more likely to model emotionally healthy behaviors that benefit themselves and those they love, including the addict. And they develop coping skills that enable them to deal with turmoil in ways that may promote healing, both for themselves and for their addicted loved one.

Families in recovery recognize that while no one can guarantee that their own recovery will help their loved one overcome addiction, no evidence exists to suggest that their prolonged misery is of any benefit to anyone. They rediscover the simple truth that their own lives have value—*independent* of the status of their loved one's addiction problems.

Strategies Supporting Recovery

Although we come to recovery only in our own time and in our own way, many families have found the following strategies to be helpful as they seek to recover from the distressing impact of coping with addiction.

Reach Out

Few experiences equal the heartbreak of watching someone you love being destroyed by alcohol or other drugs. The emotional impact can be devastating, yet the tendency of many families is to isolate and keep their suffering to themselves. After all, addiction is a disease of secrets, and families are often all too willing to join their loved one in the game of concealment.

For many, the first step along the path of recovery is reaching out for support. Although this may seem like an obvious place to start, it is actually a huge step. It requires admitting that a problem exists. Families who have denied and minimized the difficulties caused by addiction crack open the door to change when they become willing to ask for help.

We can begin finding the right support by sharing the problem with someone we trust, such as a close friend or relative who will lend a sympathetic ear. Confidants should be people who can listen without judging and who do not bombard us with unwelcome advice that will only further confuse things. One father of an alcoholic daughter recalled that his close friends were sympathetic about the situation—except for one who advised, "Put your foot down. She wouldn't get away with that in my house." The father said, "We learned who we could talk to and who we couldn't. People who don't understand the problem can say foolish things, but most of our close friends have been very supportive. They ask how she's doing. They care about our daughter, and that makes it a bit easier for us." Getting support from friends and family can help reduce the sense of isolation that so many families experience.

Support can also come from self-help groups, including Al-Anon, Nar-Anon, and other support groups that promote awareness, knowledge, and personal growth. I began attending Nar-Anon meetings soon after learning of my daughter's addiction, motivated by the desire to discover a way to "fix" her. What I found instead was a compassionate group of people who had endured the same fears, sorrow, and frustration that I was experiencing. It was in those meetings that I learned that I am not a bad person because my daughter became addicted, that I am not the only one who endured years of grinding anxiety, that other people have learned to enjoy life again despite a loved one's addiction, and (miracle of miracles!) that some families have experienced the joy of seeing their loved one recover.

In those meetings, I found the hope that my own daughter would one day become one of those miracles. For me and for countless others coping with addiction, self-help groups have become a lifeline of comfort and support. But be aware that personalities can have a powerful impact on group dynamics. If you give a group a chance but do not find it compatible with your needs, feel free to try other groups until you find one that fits. Although friends and family can offer support, they can't offer the comfort that comes only from those who have walked in your shoes.

Another important source of support is professional counseling. This is almost always useful, because families of addicts are in distress. They are dealing with something for which they are usually not prepared, and family dynamics are often strained. Guilt, blame, shame, resentment, fear, and other intense emotions can run high. Depression and anger are common. Counselors experienced in addiction can help families work through their emotions in a constructive way and provide a framework for coping with inevitable issues. Even if the addicted person or other family members are not willing to accept professional assistance, the situation can improve when even one family member gets help.

Detach with Love

As we saw earlier, detaching with love is an important tool for helping our addicted loved one. Detachment allows us to be supportive while letting go of the need to control, rescue, or judge. As a result, our addicted loved ones are free to face the consequences of their actions, an important step in breaking through the denial that sustains addiction.

But addicts aren't the only ones who benefit when we detach with love. Detachment has an equally positive impact on those of us who love an addict. When family members become wrapped up in their loved one's problems, they can lose their sense of self. They begin to suffer along with—and in some instances instead of—the addict, experiencing every jolt and crisis as intensely as if the addict's problems were their own. Unhappiness, anxiety, and depression are the result of experiencing the pain of addiction while being powerless to arrest or control the problem. Families live at the mercy of the addict, to whom they have subjugated their own identity.

This unhealthy situation can begin to improve only when families detach from their addicted loved one and once again become independent, freethinking individuals. When we detach, we learn to respond to crises with such comments as "I'm sorry to hear it. I'm sure you'll figure something out," "I know you're a capable person. You can handle this on your own," and "That's too bad." When we detach, we don't rush in to fix everything but rather allow our loved ones to solve their problems themselves. We also learn to protect ourselves by not getting drawn into conflict.

One mother said that her most useful tool for dealing with a manipulative addicted daughter was simply the word *oh*. "When she told me something I didn't believe or that upset me, I learned I didn't have to pry or react. I could just say 'oh' and leave it at that," she explained. By refusing to engage in crises and conflicts, we are not being callous or indifferent. We are simply respecting ourselves enough to live our own lives and respecting our loved ones enough to let them live theirs.

At first detachment is hard. It feels like loss. It feels like failure. It is neither. It is a simple recognition that the addict's problems and struggle are not our problems and struggle. We can offer support, encouragement, and love, but we cannot live another person's life—only our own.

Set and Keep Boundaries

"Good fences make good neighbors," wrote the poet Robert Frost—meaning that there's less room for conflict when everyone knows where the boundaries are. That's especially true for those of us who love an addict. Boundaries are those physical and emotional limits we set to let other people know how to treat us. They're lines we won't allow others to cross, designed to protect our own well-being.

They also limit the behaviors we'll accept from ourselves. When our boundaries reflect our innermost needs, beliefs, and values, we become clear about what we will and won't do.

No one will test your boundaries like an addict. Because we worry about them and know that they are sick and suffering, we tend for a time to accept behaviors in our addicted loved ones that would be intolerable in anyone else. Most families, to a greater or lesser degree, accept lies, irresponsibility, and disrespect from the addict. Some accept stealing, cheating, and destruction of property. Others accept verbal and even physical abuse. We accept these behaviors not because we are blind or weak, but because we believe that our loved ones are somehow not responsible. "It's the drink or the drug that is doing this," we rationalize.

We also accept these behaviors because we don't want to drive our loved ones away and because we fear that standing up for ourselves will only make their addiction worse. If we don't upset them, we reason, they will have less reason to go out for another drink or fix. The problem with this approach is that addicts have no limits. That's how they became addicted in the first place. Each time we allow them to cross a line, they will cross it again and again. Eventually, we can end up feeling like there is no place in our home or mind or soul that we can call our own. If we are to have a life of our own, we will have to draw the line.

I drew one line with my daughter because of her lapses into panic whenever she was faced with a crisis. Whenever she'd freak out, I'd get upset and frantically try to devise a rescue plan. After about a year of this, I'd had enough. One day we were standing in the kitchen, and she was screaming and crying about some major or minor problem. I looked at her coldly and said, "I find your behavior irritating and manipulative. It doesn't make me feel sorry for you. It just annoys me. So stop it." She quickly got herself under control.

Another woman drew the line at having syringes in her home. "Our daughter used pot and alcohol, and we were living with that because we thought we could help her," she recalled. "But when we started finding needles and drug paraphernalia in the house, we asked her to leave. We have other children at home, and we just couldn't tolerate that."

The wife of an alcoholic said, "I put up with his lies and his absence from home for days at a time. When he started stealing money out of my purse, I realized we didn't have a relationship anymore. He was just using me. I told him to leave, and I've never regretted it."

Boundaries apply not only to how we allow others to treat us, but to our own moral behavior. Addicts live in a world of shifting realities and moral ambiguities. It's easy to get drawn into the moral "squishiness" that comes with addiction. "Little" lies about why our spouse missed work can mushroom into bigger lies about why we need a prescription refill, what happened to the rent check, or who was at the wheel of the car during an accident. But the more lines we cross, the foggier we get about our own moral principles. Boundaries help us hold on to our moral moorings. When we're asked to do something that makes us uncomfortable or that just doesn't feel right, we can be guided by the limits of our own moral boundaries.

Like many people, addicts tend to do what works and what they can get away with. Sometimes people in the throes of active addiction can't prevent themselves from crossing boundaries. That is *their* problem to work on and solve as best they can. Our problem is to decide what we can and can't live with, to make our boundaries clear, and to take whatever steps are necessary to preserve our safety and sense of self-respect.

Let Go of Control, Judgment, and Expectations

Letting go of certain behaviors and attitudes can greatly increase our peace of mind, especially letting go of the need to control, letting go of passing judgment, and letting go of expectations.

Families want to control their addicted loved ones because they want to save them. Addiction destroys lives. Addiction kills. These facts haunt and terrify families, making them want to take complete control of their loved one. It can't be done, but concerned families do not give up easily. The harder they try to control things, the more stressful their situation is likely to become. Families may also cling to control because they are hooked on their own sense of power and the mistaken belief that they are the only ones who can "fix" the addiction.

"I thought that through the power of my love, wisdom, and will, I could make him give up drugs," one wife admitted.

A husband said, "I wanted her to get well, but I wanted to be the one to make it happen."

The urge to control is further heightened by the desire to escape the all-consuming anxiety that addiction can bring. If we can control the problem, we can fix it, and then we won't have to feel so awful. The sad truth is that we can't control our loved one's life, and we can't control addiction. Furthermore, when we try to exert control, we do the addict no good and only bring unhappiness and frustration to ourselves. Letting go of control is hard because we fear that things will fall apart without our interference. It helps to recognize that our efforts to control have not solved anything. It helps to remember that there are many people and events exerting influence over our loved one, and we have no way of knowing when or how circumstances will come together to bring about the miracle of recovery. It also helps to have hope that our loved one's recovery will happen in its own way and to accept that it will most likely not happen as a result of our efforts to take control.

In addition to taking control, families are often tempted to pass harsh judgments on their addicted loved ones. They want to size up the status of any recovery efforts ("He's not doing so well," "Her attitude is getting in the way," or "She's not making progress as fast as she should"). They may be highly critical if a slip or relapse occurs. But when we place ourselves in a position of judgment over others, we are judging based only on what we believe we know of them. In reality, we do not know how many times they may have resisted an opportunity to get high before they gave in to temptation. We do not know the inner turmoil and self-recrimination they may experience when they fail. And we do not know the internal workings of their minds, their fears, shame, regrets, desires, or intentions.

Even though a judgmental attitude generally stems from an anxious desire to see the addict recover, it almost always results in conflict and unhappiness. When we can see a particular occurrence as just another step in the process of change, we free ourselves from the burden of worry that things are not as they ought to be. When we stop passing judgment, we can look at our addicted loved one and see a fellow human being who is trying to cope with life as well as he or she can at that moment in time.

Finally, letting go of expectations is fundamental to recovery for most families. Only when we set aside our expectations can we stop projecting and worrying about outcomes. Many of us live on a roller coaster of hope and disappointment, fear and relief, as we try to predict what the future will bring to our addicted loved one. We pace the floor at night fearing that the worst has happened, we're flooded with happiness as a new attempt at abstinence is made, or we knot up in tension as something else goes wrong. Although emotional highs and lows are an inevitable part of coping with addiction, most of us aggravate and intensify our feelings by setting up expectations.

"I used to lie awake at night picturing my daughter dead in a Dumpster," one mother confessed. "Today, she's a computer technician and engaged to a wonderful guy who's also in recovery."

"I turned against an old friend because she didn't react the way I hoped she would when I told her about my son's addiction," another woman said. "Now I see that she wasn't wrong.

I was wrong to expect that she would react just the way I wanted."

A father said, "I always wanted a preppy son, and what I got was a kid with piercings, tattoos, and a serious drug problem. I love him anyway, but to arrive at unconditional love, I had to let go of a lot of expectations."

Letting go of expecting that people should live up to our standards—and of projecting that things will or won't turn out as we hope—allows us to live more consciously in the present. When we let go of expectations, we are better able to appreciate what is good in the here and now.

Focus on Yourself

Of all the recovery tools for families of addicts, perhaps none presents a greater challenge than focusing on ourselves. This may be because it feels selfish to put ourselves first when we are used to taking care of others. It may also be because many of us don't know who our "self" is anymore.

"When people told me to focus on myself, I thought they were nuts," one woman exclaimed. "I didn't know who I was, so there was nothing for me to focus on unless I was looking after my son."

Another woman said that she had abandoned all of her interests over the years as she became increasingly preoccupied with her son's addiction problems. "I used to love to do crafts and sewing," she said. "I made some beautiful things. But I stopped all that when his problems started."

A father said, "I didn't even know what I believed in or stood for, because I'd spent so much time covering up and making excuses for my daughter."

In its deepest sense, focusing on ourselves gives us the opportunity to discover or reaffirm who we really are. When we stop looking outward and start looking inward, we can begin to explore the many facets of our essential being: what we truly feel, what we actually enjoy, and what we really believe in. Focusing on ourselves allows us to clarify our goals, dreams, interests, and values, a process that may involve trying new activities, meeting new people, and learning new things. It can also mean reconnecting with people and places we used to enjoy but abandoned over the years.

Whatever direction focusing on ourselves takes us, it can, at first, be extremely uncomfortable. We may experience turbulent emotions, such as anger, resentment, and guilt, if we have buried our feelings in concern about our loved one. We may experience a sense of emptiness if we have directed all our energies to trying to help him or her. We may also feel oddly disoriented, because it is much easier to see how others should live their lives than it is to see how we should live our own.

Yet our own life is the only one that we truly have to work with, the only one that is absolutely ours to control. It is a gift and no less precious, no less valuable, than the life of our addicted loved one. When we put the focus on ourselves, we are not turning our back on others in need or giving up on our responsibility to someone we love. We are simply choosing to cherish this one life that is ours to live to the very best of our ability.

A Journey, Not a Destination

To follow a path of recovery is to embrace the concept that growth and change are a natural part of life. There is never a point when we can say that we are fully recovered or that the process is complete. Even well into recovery, emotional and mental health problems may persist. Difficult personality traits may continue to be a challenge. And the possibility of relapse is never completely eradicated.

Still, for addicts and their families, a life in recovery is a life of growth and possibility. One special reward of recovery is the opportunity to heal the wounds we carry and to emerge with a greater measure of wisdom and serenity. In the next chapter, we will look at what this process of healing can mean.

NINE

A Time to Heal

"In the midst of winter, I found there was,
within me, an invincible summer."
—ALBERT CAMUS

ONE FINE SPRING MORNING many years ago, Jane dropped off her two small children at their babysitter's house. Then she went home and, with her boyfriend, loaded all her household possessions into a U-Haul truck. The drug-addicted couple was bound for Florida, and although they didn't get far, that act of abandonment initiated eight years of estrangement between Jane and her children. During that painful period, the children lived with their grandparents as their mother sank ever deeper into a life of drug use, rehab, relapse, and imprisonment. What confusion, hurt, and sorrow the children endured can well be imagined, as can their mother's shame, guilt, and bitter sense of loss.

Yet after eight years of being drug- and alcohol-free, Jane and her children enjoyed a dream vacation in Hawaii—a family getaway that included her son and daughter-in-law and her daughter and her daughter's boyfriend. The family spent nine days sightseeing, relaxing on the beach, and talking and playing together.

"It's a miracle," said Jane, who once survived a frigid winter by sleeping in cellars. "My life today is truly a miracle. Not that everything is perfect. My daughter still has a lot of anger at me.

The hurt is still there, even though a lot of healing has taken place."

Jane's relationship with her mother is beginning to heal as well. She explained, "My parents disowned me during those years. When I got my first-year coin [an AA award for sobriety], my mother just said, 'That's good. Get one next year.' The second year it was the same thing because she was afraid to trust. But the third year she went to my meeting with me and gave me my coin. And my sister just gave me my eight-year coin." She paused and added, "Healing takes time. I think it's a lifelong process."

Mark, a recovering alcoholic, echoed that sentiment. "Healing is ongoing," he said. "We haven't 'arrived.' It's not a place where you go and everything's all better. I still make mistakes. I still have bad days. Everybody does. But I also have peace, and that's what healing is all about for me. Making peace with the past and being able to appreciate the present."

His words capture the essence of the concept of healing: being able to appreciate what is good and beautiful in life even as we acknowledge the presence of suffering. It's the process of putting things to rest piece by piece and attaining a stable sense of inner serenity.

A serene state of mind can seem unattainable to families who are embroiled in the trauma of active addiction. Even when families are actively seeking their own recovery, they may wonder why things don't seem to get better. They may practice detachment, set personal boundaries, build a network of support, and try to develop their own individual interests—yet they may still be burdened with a host of unhappy feelings including anxiety, sadness, guilt, anger, resentment, and shame. They may still feel the pain of addiction dragging them down.

The truth is that the tools of recovery can open the door to a better way of life, but healing itself is a gradual, ongoing evolution of emotional and spiritual growth. Healing takes time, along with the desire and willingness to nurture our own personal well-being. The following strategies are often helpful in nurturing that growth.

Choosing to Heal

Addiction cuts deep into the fabric of family relationships. Trust is broken. Expectations are shattered. The accumulation of worry, disappointment, and heartache takes its toll. It is not uncommon for family members to wonder if they will ever be capable of experiencing happiness again.

Hope, whose daughter repeatedly broke her heart, said, "For years I felt dead inside. I thought of myself as a flower that had withered away and died. Only very gradually did I come to see that I could continue to wallow in my pain or I could choose to begin the healing process. I had to heal if I ever wanted a better quality of life. For me, healing started when I made the choice not to be a victim but instead to be responsible for me."

As many families have found, we don't have to wait until our loved one starts to get better before we can begin our own healing process. As Hope put it, "Healing is about us, not about our addicts. Our loved ones have their own journeys to make in their own time. If we really want to heal, to stop hurting inside, we have to start making choices that support our intention. We have to believe we have a right to a happy life."

Elaine agreed. "My daughter called us last week and said that she'd had a relapse. She's living with a guy who's actively using, and she picked up again. She cried about it, but she said she wasn't ready to try to get clean. I felt terrible after hearing the news. But I was able to sleep that night. Because I've learned how to make my own peace of mind a priority, I'm better able to accept whatever life brings."

Both Hope and Elaine have discovered that healing is a choice. It begins with the conscious decision to create a happier life for ourselves. When we choose to heal, we recognize that we—no less than anyone else—are deserving of contentment and peace of mind. Often, contentment begins with the simple willingness to accept life as it is.

Practicing Acceptance

As families of addicts, we have devoted a lot of energy to struggling against what is. Just as addiction itself is an escape from reality, we've lived in denial, pretended that things are not what they are, and fought mightily to change what we have no power to change. The constant battle is not only exhausting—it's futile. For reality is always just that: reality. Despite all our protests, despite our passionate insistence that things should be different, life is what it is. By learning to accept this fundamental truth, the energy that we've expended so fruitlessly on denial and pretense can be channeled into pathways of healing and growth.

Jack, whose son was addicted to crack for many years, explained how acceptance has changed his life. "I just couldn't accept that he was an addict, that he stole from me, that he was actually in prison," he recalled. "I mean, I knew it, but part of me couldn't accept it without being overcome by rage or grief. Part of me was always fighting against it. It took a long time before I could finally accept what had happened in our lives, before I could say, 'This is how things are. I have no choice. They are what they are.' I didn't have to like them. I didn't have to understand them. I just needed to accept them. When I finally did, I felt this great sense of calm come over me that has never completely gone away."

Jack also had to learn to accept other previously unpalatable realities. "Another hard thing for me to accept was that my dreams for my son would most likely never come true," he said. "His life didn't follow the course I'd imagined it would, and I felt a real sense of loss, even betrayal, before I came to acceptance. He is who he is. He'll probably always have struggles. But my acceptance of that doesn't make me love him any less."

For Hope, acceptance centered around her relationship with her daughter. "When my daughter was still using, I had to accept that I might never have a close relationship with her," she said. "I'm not sure it's possible to have a real relationship with someone who is actively using. I also had to accept the fact that she might die without being healed. That was a tough one, but it was a reality."

Deb, whose husband has battled addiction for years, said, "We don't fight as much as we used to. I just get sad now because this will never end. He will always be an addict, yet I will always love him. I sometimes grieve for the things, and the life, that I will never have. Children are quite out of the question, and sometimes that makes me sad. But I have come to accept it."

Perhaps the fundamental reality that we must come to accept is that we have control over no one's life but our own. Hope summed it up by saying, "It took me a long time to see that I alone am responsible for who I am as a person. For years, I believed that if I could make someone else into the person I wanted them to be, I'd be okay. Now I see that taking care of my own life is the most I can do. And that is quite enough."

Acceptance—the essential antidote to denial—does not imply that change is not desirable or possible. It does not signal defeat. It is not the end of hopes and dreams. It simply means that we recognize and accept the reality of our lives as they actually are at this moment in time.

Living in the Present

It seems to be human nature to spend much of our mental existence either fretting about the past or worrying about the future. Yet many families who have healed from the effects of addiction have found that living in the present is central to their peace of mind. When we live in the present, we focus our attention on the here and now. We learn to let go of the endless recycling of anxious thoughts about the past or future, freeing ourselves to appreciate what is good and nurturing in the present moment.

Living this way is hard to do, but as Deb expressed it, "I don't have power over the past or future. I only have this present moment, one day at a time. I can choose to make this day the very best I can or choose to waste it on things over which I have no control. When I am burdened by memories, or when I start projecting about what might or might not happen tomorrow, I try to get my mind back to the here and now."

Jack said that he too draws strength from living in the present: "My son's clean right now, but last week he said he had a desire to use. I know that relapse could be just a moment away, but I don't let my mind go there. I work really hard to stay in the day. That's the only way I can stay healthy."

Learning to Forgive

For most families, forgiveness is a key element of healing. As long as we harbor anger or guilt in our hearts, we are allowing ourselves to be victims of addiction. The negative feelings gnaw away at us, diminishing our capacity to fully experience what is good and worthwhile in life.

Anger is a natural response when we suffer. We look to blame someone or something for our unhappiness and end up feeling angry at the person—our addicted loved one—who has caused us pain, or at society, or even at God, if we have a Higher Power in our lives. Unfortunately, anger does not make us feel better. It only adds to the pain we are already feeling.

Deb recalled, "I used to get physically sick from resentment and anger. I used to feel so sorry for myself because I had married an addict and didn't have what everyone else had. Then I'd take it out on him and pick these huge fights. I really struggled with forgiveness for a long time. I still do. But I've decided that forgiving others is not a feeling. It's a decision. I can't manufacture it. It's a gift, but it starts with making the decision."

Hope, too, struggled with forgiveness. "I used to cry out to God, 'Why have you done this to me? Why have you abandoned me?' I have always been a very spiritual person. I have a strong faith. But for a long time, I was angry with God for allowing this to happen to my daughter. I was also so angry with her that I didn't talk to her for almost a year. She was in jail, and I refused to take her calls. I couldn't get past all the things she had done to me and her kids."

Forgiveness has been essential to Hope's healing process. She said, "My daughter is a changed person today. She is very active in NA and AA. We went out to lunch last week, and she made her amends to me. Did it make the past go away? No. What's done is done. But unless I chose to accept that and let the past go, there would always be a wedge between us. I didn't want that. Forgiveness is an act. Even if you don't feel it, you can say it. My main goal is not to get my addict well, but to get me well—not get her well and make myself sick in the process. Forgiveness is critical, not for the other person, but for yourself."

Hope added, "Forgiveness is an important part of any relationship. You have to stay on top of things so resentments don't build up. Days ago, I got angry at my daughter because she didn't do something I wanted her to do. I realized I was wrong and told her I was sorry."

Some families find it easier to forgive their addicted loved one than to forgive themselves. That has been my experience. Although I have certainly had flashes of anger toward my daughter, my overriding feelings toward her have been sorrow and love mingled with a good deal of self-recrimination. Looking back, I can see that I was not always a good parent, and although she has forgiven me, I have struggled to forgive myself. In this I am not alone. For example, Jack said that his healing process has included "admitting that I had a part to play in what happened to my son." According to him, "I felt a lot of self-blame. It's been tough to get past that."

Forgiving ourselves can be hard to do when we fear our actions have profoundly hurt someone we love. Jane said, "I felt a great deal of guilt and shame about the things I did that hurt my kids. I couldn't even say to them I was sorry because it was so much bigger than that. All I could do was just show up, be responsible, be there for them the way I should have been all along. I'm paying for college for my daughter. I'm doing everything I can to be a good mother to her and my son. Do I forgive myself? I'm working on it."

Some families continually beat themselves up because they fear they haven't done as much as they could have to save their loved one from addiction. They find it hard to forgive themselves for failing to do the impossible—getting another person clean and sober. Accepting responsibility for our mistakes and doing our best to make amends to those we have hurt is important. However, holding on to self-blame damages our sense of self-worth and limits our ability to heal.

Hope finds it helpful to put things in perspective when it comes to self-forgiveness. "I did the best I could for the time I was in," she said. "I am not perfect. I think a lot of us tend to be too hard on ourselves. I think we should be more gentle and stop beating ourselves up. If God can forgive us, we should be able to forgive ourselves."

Hope's words echo a well-known truth: "To err is human; to forgive, divine."

Practicing Mindfulness

Mindfulness is as relevant today as it was when it was introduced by the Buddha more than 2,500 years ago. Research has shown it to be an effective tool for fostering overall well-being, and health professionals are increasingly recommending it to patients who want to improve their mental, emotional, and physical health.

There are many ways to define *mindfulness,* but one of my favorites is contained in The Mindfulness Project's book *I Am Here Now:* "Mindfulness is the simple and very powerful practice of training our attention. It's simple in that it's really just about paying attention to what's happening here and now (i.e., sensations, thoughts, and emotions) in a nonjudgmental way. It's powerful because it can interrupt the habit of getting lost in thoughts, mostly about the future or past, which often generates more stress on top of the real pressures of everyday life."

When we practice mindfulness, we gradually become more aware of the reality around us, more accepting of life as it is, and more compassionate toward ourselves and others. We build a foundation of healthy detachment that frees us from the unhappiness of clinging to our desires or obsessing about our fears. Just as detachment from our addicted loved one is essential for our peace of mind, detachment in a broader sense allows us to accept with equanimity the changes that life inevitably brings.

Although the *concept* of mindfulness is simple, in reality it's hard to be mindful. Our mind naturally wanders, we make up stories that we accept as truth, and we view just about everything through the lens of judgment. Because mindfulness involves training the mind to process information differently, it requires practice—hence the phrase *practicing mindfulness*.

There are many ways to practice mindfulness, but one of the easiest ways to get started is to focus on the breath. Periodically throughout the day—whenever you feel your mind start to race or notice negative thoughts entering your head—turn your attention to the natural inhalation and exhalation of your breath. Doing this for even five complete breathing cycles can help calm your mind. To dig deeper into mindfulness, consider adding meditation to your daily routine or enrolling in a course that teaches specific mindfulness techniques.

Developing Your Spirituality

Spirituality, as it applies to healing from the effects of addiction, does not necessarily include having a Higher Power in our lives, although it can. It simply means taking steps to awaken the core of joy that is present in all human beings from the moment of birth. This may involve religion, nature, art, music, literature, helping others, or following any other life-affirming pursuit that connects us to something greater than ourselves. For me, spirituality is nurtured through the practice of mindfulness, devoting a few minutes every day to sitting meditation and other reflective practices.

However we define or access it, spirituality involves taking time to connect with something bigger than our narrow scope of worries and concerns. It frees us to experience life on a deeper, grander level. When we are consumed with anxiety about our addicted loved one, our openness to the world shrivels. We tend to overlook what is beautiful in life and focus narrowly on what is frightening or tragic. Then we may conclude that the world is a terrible place or, at the very least, that our destiny is to suffer. One woman said, "I only see the bad in things. If I think about my son's future, I see him winding up on the streets and eating out of Dumpsters. It never enters my mind to think that he might get better and live a wonderful life."

A husband said about his wife, "I worry constantly that she might start drinking again, even though she's been good for almost a year now. I can't appreciate her sobriety because I'm too afraid she's going to relapse."

Negative thoughts are inevitable in families of addicts. We've had a lot of negative experiences. It is easy for us to lose our faith and hope. If we are to heal, we must counteract the negative by nurturing our spirit. For Deb, this involved becoming active in a local theater group. "I love acting," she said. "Playing other characters helps me see how much there really is to life, how we all have our struggles. It helps put my own problems into perspective."

For Jack, developing his spirituality included taking long hikes in the mountains: "I'd always loved hiking, but I gave it up somehow or another. Now I try to get a good hike in at least once a week. There's something special about a view from a mountaintop. You get a sense that some things will last forever. I feel peace up there."

Hope's spiritual growth stemmed from strengthening her conscious contact with God. "God is a part of my everyday life now," she said. "I talk to him every day, and I trust him to take care of me and those I love. I have to listen and wait for his guidance. It can come in unexpected ways. For example, I remember sitting in a Nar-Anon meeting one night, feeling depressed as usual. A woman in the group was very funny, and she said something that made everyone laugh. I laughed too, and then I thought, 'Oh my God, I'm laughing. Maybe I'm not dead inside after all.' I hadn't laughed in years. Laughing felt strange, but it gave me a glimmer of light. I thought that maybe God wanted something more for me than to waste my life in self-pity. My advice to anyone who wants to heal is to trust any awakening you feel and keep building on it."

By trusting those glimmers of light and nurturing the things that give meaning and beauty to our lives, we help our spirits to heal and grow.

Healing Lessons

Someday far down the road, when the pain of facing addiction is not so raw and when we have begun our journey toward recovery and healing, we may come to regard the addiction of our loved one as a turning point that led us to embrace life on a deeper level. Every crisis presents an opportunity for personal growth, and facing the addiction of a loved one can help us to become stronger, more tolerant, and less judgmental.

As Jack expressed it, "I would never say I'm glad my son became addicted. But I'm thankful that as a result of his addiction, I've become a better person. There was a time when I might have looked at others who were having family problems and thought, 'What are you doing wrong? You must have done something to cause this.' Now I'm more compassionate. I know that terrible trouble can come to anyone."

Deb said, "I used to be very judgmental. I couldn't understand why people didn't just do things my way. Then everything would be all right. Now I believe that everyone is doing the best they can. You can't expect more than that."

Hope said, "Because addiction came into my life, I've become a little more accepting of other people, a little more understanding of what other people are feeling. It's also helped me put things in perspective. I don't have a lot of tolerance for the 'poor me' syndrome anymore. Instead of dwelling on what's not here, I keep a gratitude list. Sometime it's an exercise to say, 'I trust you, God.' But I have faith. I have some peace. This is life."

What Jack, Deb, Hope, and many others have learned is that addiction is a devastating experience both for addicted individuals and for those who love them. Few things in life are more painful than watching addiction steal our loved ones away from us. But addiction is also an experience from which addicts and their families can emerge stronger and wiser than they were before. Many recovering addicts, including my own daughter, become people of great compassion, humility, and generosity. Many recovering families of addicts develop similar strengths of character.

Addiction is not a disease that can be completely cured. Like many chronic conditions, it can recur, sometimes when we least expect it. Nevertheless, addiction is a disease from which important lessons can be learned. If from among those lessons we learn how to live our own lives to the best of our ability and acquire the grace to allow others to do the same, then something immeasurably precious will have been won.

Common Addictive Substances: Effects and Signs of Use

All psychoactive substances achieve their effects by changing the chemical balance in the brain's reward center, a circuit of chemical messengers and electrical impulses that produces feelings of pleasure. When we do something enjoyable, our reward center releases dopamine, endorphins, and other neurotransmitters—miniscule messenger chemicals—that carry messages of pleasure, calm, and euphoria. The chemical messengers then connect with targeted receptors that fire off a pleasurable sensation. Addictive substances replicate these feelings, either by mimicking the brain's own pleasure messenger chemicals or by overstimulating the reward center to release more pleasure messenger chemicals.

The following chemicals are major players in the addiction process.

Dopamine
A neurotransmitter that is plentiful in the brain's reward circuit. It is the brain's primary pleasure messenger.

Endorphins
These morphine-like neurotransmitters reduce pain, alleviate stress, and promote pleasure.

Gamma-Aminobutyric Acid (GABA)
This neurotransmitter quiets the brain by blocking stimulation, including anxiety and worry.

Norepinephrine
Similar to adrenaline, this neurotransmitter affects heart rate and blood pressure and is involved in the body's natural fight-or-flight response to emergencies.

Serotonin
This chemical affects motor function, pain perception, appetite, and the sympathetic nervous system, which is not subject to voluntary control.

Some drugs, such as marijuana, heroin, and narcotic painkillers, contain compounds whose structure is similar to that of dopamine and endorphins, the pleasure-producing neurotransmitters. In the brain, these substances mimic their naturally occurring counterparts, and users experience calm, contentment, and euphoria.

Other drugs, such as cocaine and methamphetamine, trick the brain's reward center into releasing abnormally large amounts of neurotransmitters—primarily dopamine—or stop the normal recycling process in which neurotransmitters are reabsorbed by the brain. As a result, dopamine and other pleasure messenger chemicals flood the brain, and the user experiences feelings of energy, alertness, confidence, and an exaggerated sense of well-being.

The pleasurable effects of psychoactive substances are profound but generally short-term. And because the brain always strives to achieve a balance, when the initial effects begin to wear off, the exact opposite effects begin to occur. Withdrawal from a depressant will generally produce agitation, and withdrawal from a stimulant will lead to exhaustion. Addicts must use a drug with regularity to sustain the pleasurable effects of the drug and avoid the negative effects of withdrawal.

Following is an overview of the major psychoactive addictive substances widely available today. This listing contains a simplified account of the chemical properties of each substance, its effects on the user, symptoms of use and withdrawal, and paraphernalia associated with its use.

Alcohol

Alcohol is produced by a chemical reaction between fermenting enzymes (most often from yeast) and sugars or starches from plant products. The enzymes split complex organic matter (sugar) into simple substances (carbon dioxide and alcohol). Fermentation naturally stops when the alcohol concentration in the mixture reaches a level that kills the yeast, usually around 12 to 14 percent.

A much higher concentration of alcohol is achieved through the process of distillation. Heating fermented products to create vapors and then cooling and collecting the vapors makes whiskey, gin, rum, and other hard liquors. A drink's label lists the percentage of alcohol by volume (abbreviated as "% ABV") it contains. In the United States, labels may also list a drink's "proof." The proof number is twice the percentage of alcohol in a given liquor. Thus, 90-proof whiskey is 45 percent alcohol.

Beer, wine, and hard liquors all contain the same type of alcohol: pure ethyl alcohol. Although some beer or wine drinkers believe that their drinks are less intoxicating than mixed drinks, they are mistaken. A twelve-ounce glass of beer, about five ounces of wine, and about one-and-a-half ounces of distilled liquor contain equivalent amounts of alcohol: about one-half ounce. Furthermore, the short-term and long-term effects of these drinks are the same.

Although alcohol immediately acts as a stimulant, it is in fact a depressant drug. The initial alcohol high is caused by a surge of dopamine, serotonin, epinephrine (related to norepinephrine), and endorphins. Alcohol also stimulates the release of GABA. The result of this chemical cocktail is a sensation of warmth and well-being and a lessening of inhibitions, which explains why people under the influence will often do or say things they later find embarrassing. Suppressed inhibitions may lead drinkers to display unusual affection, express grandiose ideas, or become noticeably hostile. Eventually, the quieting effects of GABA will cause drinkers to feel sleepy. But heavy alcohol consumption disrupts normal brain function, leading to anxiety, sleeplessness, and nightmares as withdrawal sets in.

Alcohol in low doses is generally harmless, although the artificially induced sense of well-being may impair judgment and slow reflex time, leading to serious accidents. Additionally, habitual drinking of even small doses can eventually lead to the release of anger and irritability. It is not uncommon for routine evening drinkers to unleash their dissatisfaction with the world as the alcohol strips away their inhibitions. In larger doses, alcohol affects motor skills, causing loss of coordination and slurred speech; irritates the stomach lining; and triggers the body's vomiting mechanism.

Another consequence of heavy drinking is a blackout, an episode in which the drinker looks and acts relatively normal but is highly intoxicated. The drinker will later have no memory of what was done or said during that period. A single episode of heavy drinking can also produce loss of consciousness, a coma, or even death.

There is no precise measure of the difference between harmless social drinking, excessive drinking, and alcoholism (full-blown addiction). One guideline suggests that the "safe" number of drinks per week is seven for women and eleven for men. In his book *The Selfish Brain,* Dr. Robert L. DuPont says that routinely having more than four drinks a week may be cause for concern. Regardless of the quantity of alcohol consumed, when alcohol produces changed moods and behaviors or blackouts, and when it begins to interfere with daily life, a line has been crossed; the drinking has become problematic and should be treated.

Not all problem drinkers exhibit the more obvious signs of alcohol abuse. I have known people who regularly consume a six-pack or more of sixteen-ounce beers every night and yet show no outward signs of intoxication. This is not remarkable among heavy drinkers. Most alcoholics can "hold their liquor"; that is, they exhibit only minor effects from heavy drinking. They have conditioned their brains to function reasonably well with alcohol present. This learned condition causes many heavy drinkers to believe that alcohol does not affect them. But prolonged heavy use of alcohol takes its toll whether or not the effects are immediately apparent.

The physical consequences of long-term alcohol abuse begin with the liver, where alcohol is broken down into carbon dioxide and water. The liver can be damaged in three progressively serious ways: (1) normal red liver tissue is replaced with yellow fat; (2) liver hepatitis develops, which means that the inflamed liver malfunctions, leading to yellowing of the eyes and skin (jaundice); or (3) cirrhosis of the liver occurs, in which normal tissue is replaced by white scar tissue. The cirrhotic liver cannot do its job of cleaning the blood, and this leads to blood poisoning and other life-threatening conditions. Cirrhosis of the liver is nonreversible, although the progress of the disease may stop if drinking ceases. In its advanced stages, cirrhosis is fatal.

In addition to liver disease, long-term heavy drinking produces other physical impairments. Alcohol often irritates the gastrointestinal tract and can inflame the esophagus and stomach, aggravating peptic ulcer disease. It can inflame the pancreas, leading to chronic acute pancreatitis. This condition produces a knife-like pain in the middle abdomen and can be fatal. Alcoholism can result in permanent brain degeneration, including paralysis of nerves and memory loss. It can also lead to anemia, cardiovascular diseases, and degeneration of the heart muscle. As if all this were not enough, alcohol abuse also contributes to cancer of the mouth, esophagus, stomach, larynx, liver, and lung. Babies born to alcoholic mothers often suffer from fetal alcohol spectrum disorder (FASD), a combination of permanent physical and mental defects.

Habitual heavy drinkers may experience severe withdrawal if they abruptly stop drinking. This potentially fatal condition, known as delirium tremens (DTs), may induce high fever, hallucinations, and seizures.

Alcoholism is a progressive disease that causes severe physical and mental damage over time. Early indicators of alcohol abuse, in addition to the well-recognized effects of intoxication, include alcohol odor on the breath or excreted by sweat glands, bleary eyes, chronic stomachaches or pain, facial yellowing and/or puffiness, shakiness and irritability in the mornings, loss of appetite, frequent accidents, blackouts, and sudden and inexplicable mood swings.

Evidence of use: a steady stock of alcohol in the house, empty cans or bottles, hidden cans or bottles—full or empty.

Marijuana

Marijuana consists of the flowering tops, leaves, and stems of the plant *Cannabis sativa*. Unlike alcohol, cocaine, and heroin, which are refined agricultural products consisting of a single chemical, marijuana is used in its crude, natural state. The dried plant contains more than 420 different chemicals, while marijuana smoke contains more than 2,000. The chemical most responsible for the marijuana high is delta-9-tetrahydrocannabinol (THC). THC receptors are widely distributed throughout the brain, with higher concentrations in the cerebellum and hippocampus, regions involved with motor function, learning, and memory. The brain's pleasure centers are connected to these areas, but scientists have yet to determine the natural function of the neurotransmitter that matches THC. It is known that THC stimulates the norepinephrine transmitter system, and there are indications that it may also affect levels of GABA and serotonin.

Although the precise mechanics of the marijuana high are still unclear, the effects of using marijuana are well documented. The drug sedates the brain and alters mental processes. The ability to learn, concentrate, and remember is diminished; reaction time is slowed; and perception of time and distance is distorted. Appetite and thirst may increase, and in larger doses, marijuana may induce irritability, paranoia, anxiety, and panic.

When used during pregnancy, marijuana has been linked to lower birth weight and brain and behavioral problems in babies and small children. According to NIDA, people who regularly use large quantities of marijuana report "lower life satisfaction, poorer mental health, poorer physical health, and more relationship problems" than their nonusing peers.

Marijuana is usually smoked, though edibles have become increasingly popular as more states have legalized the consumption of marijuana. Because THC is fat soluble and not water soluble, it is not easily eliminated from the body but is instead retained in the brain, reproductive glands, and other fat-containing tissues of the body for days or even weeks. Studies have shown that the retained THC can impair memory for six weeks or longer after marijuana is used.

There is some debate about whether marijuana is technically an addictive drug, since it generally produces no physical withdrawal symptoms. There is no question, however, that heavy marijuana use leads to physical and psychological dependence and that compulsive use of the drug can persist despite severe negative consequences.

Evidence of use: small seeds, stems, and leaves resembling dried basil; pipes, bongs (water pipes), and rolling paper (sold for rolling cigarettes but usually used for rolling joints); small, flattened remains of marijuana cigarettes (roaches); ash that does not smell like tobacco; burn holes in clothing, bedding, furniture, or car seats; the distinctive smell of marijuana smoke; dilated pupils and bloodshot eyes.

Cocaine

Cocaine is made from coca leaves native to South America. To isolate the active ingredient, producers soak the leaves and mash them into a paste, which is 60 to 80 percent pure cocaine. It is generally distributed in salt form, a fine white powder that resembles snow. Users snort it through their nose, rub it on their gums, or dissolve it in water and inject it.

In the 1980s, a more potent form of the drug, crack cocaine, was developed, using a process that produces rock crystals. The rocks or pellets are heated with a flame to produce vapors that are inhaled. High levels of crack hit the brain within eight seconds of being smoked, delivering the fastest and most powerful high of any drug. (Drugs used intravenously reach the brain in about sixteen seconds.)

Because a cocaine high is so fleeting, lasting less than an hour, the drug is usually taken in "runs." Users take repeated hits every few minutes for hours or even days. They pursue their initial euphoria with manic compulsion. However, with each repeated use, the high becomes less and less satisfying.

Cocaine, like all stimulant drugs, affects the body's central nervous system, increasing heart rate and blood pressure. It triggers the release of norepinephrine and promotes sensations of alertness, confidence, and energy. But cocaine's real kick comes from its effects on the dopamine system.

Most dopamine neurotransmitters cycle through the brain again and again. A few of them, however, are broken down by naturally occurring enzymes, and the body gradually creates new dopamine to replace them and maintain a balance. This natural process is disrupted by cocaine, which keeps dopamine in circulation for an abnormally long time, causing euphoria and an exaggerated sensation of well-being. As the brain gets locked in this supercharged state, sleep becomes impossible and hunger is suppressed.

Sensing that dopamine is at an unusually high concentration, the natural enzymes begin to break it down in large quantities, faster than it can be replaced. Dopamine loss sets in. By the time the cocaine run stops, little dopamine is left in the brain. The user feels tired and often intensely depressed. The brain can take months to re-establish a normal dopamine balance, and prolonged heavy cocaine abuse may permanently damage the dopamine system, diminishing the addict's capacity to experience any pleasure at all.

Among substances of abuse, cocaine is distinctive because of its diminishing returns. Most addicts of other substances start using to achieve the euphoric feelings associated with initial use; however, they continue using in order to feel "normal." Heavy cocaine use never creates a feeling of normalcy. Instead, it causes panic, paranoia, aggression, and not uncommonly, psychotic episodes. It distorts judgment and twists perceptions, effects that can last for weeks or even months after it was last used. Some users experience "coke bugs," a disturbing sensation that bugs are burrowing under their skin. They may try to dig them out with their fingernails, creating open sores on their bodies. Babies born to crack-addicted mothers often suffer severe developmental handicaps.

Cocaine produces no clearly defined withdrawal symptoms, and users are not compelled to use their drug daily, unlike alcoholics and heroin addicts. But it is highly addictive. The compulsion to use becomes irresistible, and the search for the cocaine high becomes so compelling that most addicts can't stop until their world crashes down around them.

Evidence of use: plastic baggies; fine, white powder that numbs the tongue if tasted; bullets, or specially made devices that are used to measure out a dose of cocaine and fit into the nostrils; pea-size brownish pellets (crack); crack pipes, often made by sticking a straw in a plastic bottle and placing tinfoil on the open end; blackened fingernails and decayed front teeth (indicates crack use); constantly running nose (indicates cocaine use); wads of tissues or paper towels in pockets (for runny nose); nonstop talking; physical agitation; extreme lethargy.

Heroin

Heroin is morphine (a narcotic derived from opium poppies) combined with two activating chemicals (acetyl groups) that speed up the drug's entry into the brain. Once in the brain, the acetyl groups fall off, leaving the morphine molecules to work their effects. (Morphine, not heroin, is found in urine tests of heroin users.) Street heroin is combined with nonactive substances such as starch, powdered milk, sugar, or quinine. It is a soft, fine powder resembling talc and ranging in color from off-white to dark brown. It is commonly sold in approximately one-by-two-inch bags of opaque paper. The bags are sealed on both ends and up the back and stamped on the front with a colored pattern, the dealer's stamp.

Heroin is usually injected intravenously, although purer, more potent forms of the drug now make it possible to get high by snorting it. Snorting is how many people today are introduced to heroin because snorting does not carry the same stigma as intravenous drug use. As addiction takes hold, however, most users graduate to the more powerful method of injecting.

To prepare for intravenous use, the user dissolves the heroin by adding it to water in a spoon or bottle cap, then heating it with a match or lighter. To prevent undissolved particles from entering the bloodstream, users may place cotton or a piece of cigarette filter in the liquid before drawing it up into the needle.

Whether snorted or injected, heroin stimulates the release of dopamine and acts directly on the brain's natural opioid receptors (the endorphin system). The result is a sensation of warmth, a powerful rush of pleasure followed by a sense of calm and contentment (inexperienced users may vomit with initial heroin use, but this reaction disappears as tolerance develops). Heroin, like all opioid-based substances, eases pain and distress by inhibiting the transmission of pain-carrying impulses. As a depressant, it affects most major systems of the body. It slows the respiratory system, lowers blood pressure, suppresses coughs, slows bowel function (leading to constipation), reduces appetite and sex drive, minimizes aggression, and interferes with normal menstrual cycles.

The immediate effect of heroin is a warm glow. The user's face may be flushed and shiny, the nose and eyes may be runny, and the pupils may be constricted. Severe itching may also occur. A pleasant, languid drowsiness takes hold, causing the user to "nod," a condition resembling sleep in which the upper eyelids droop and the mouth hangs open. This phase is followed by a period of calm during which there are few observable changes in the user's appearance or behavior. Unlike abusers of alcohol, marijuana, and cocaine, heroin addicts can use for a long time before being detected if they have access to a steady supply of their drug.

The effects of heroin last for several hours before withdrawal begins. Because it is physically addictive and affects every part of the body, even the bones, heroin withdrawal is extremely unpleasant. Addicts experience nausea, severe aches and pains, sweating, insomnia, panic, depression, cramping, and diarrhea. Their behavior becomes anxious and agitated as they begin their search for the next fix.

Heroin withdrawal, unlike alcohol, benzodiazepine, or barbiturate withdrawal, is rarely life-threatening. Nevertheless, heroin addiction can have serious consequences, including death from overdose. The risk of overdose has greatly increased with the introduction of synthetic opioids like fentanyl into the illegal drug market. Fentanyl—which is sometimes mixed with cocaine and methamphetamine as well as heroin—is 50 to 100 times more potent than morphine. According to the National Institute on Drug Abuse, "Synthetic opioids, including fentanyl, are now the most common drugs involved in drug overdose deaths in the United States."

The risk of overdose also increases after a period of abstinence, which lowers addicts' tolerance level. Doses that they could previously tolerate may now prove lethal. Other health risks include HIV infection from sharing needles, collapsed veins from repeated injections, serious infections at injection sites, and hepatitis, an incurable and potentially fatal disease that damages the liver. Pregnant users risk miscarriages and stillbirths, and infants who do survive are born addicted and experience painful withdrawal symptoms.

Evidence of use: off-white or brownish bitter-tasting powder; scabs and scarring on veins, especially on the arms and hands; "kits" or "works" consisting of a syringe, a spoon or bottle cap, a tourniquet (to enlarge veins for injection), matches or a lighter, and cotton balls or cigarette filters that are shredded or cut into disks; tissues with blood spots; spots of blood on inner sleeves or cuffs; cigarette holes on clothes, bedding, car seats, or furniture (from smoking while nodding); flushed face; constricted pupils; watery eyes and nose; itching; extreme lethargy or agitation.

In addition to the four major addictive substances, there are many other natural and synthetic substances that alter brain chemistry. Here is a brief overview of the most common.

Prescription Drugs
Prescription drug abuse has skyrocketed in the United States since the 1990s. Stimulants such as Ritalin (most commonly prescribed to treat attention-deficit/hyperactivity disorder) and sedatives such as Klonopin and other benzodiazepines (most commonly prescribed to treat anxiety and intended for short-term use) have a high potential for diversion and misuse. Benzodiazepines are highly addictive and, when used with alcohol or opioids, can lead to overdose. Opioid pain relievers are also widely misused and are implicated in the sharp rise in opioid addiction and overdose deaths across the country. The federal government has taken steps to curtail the overprescribing of opioids that was rampant from 2000 through 2015, but prescription opioid misuse continues to be a significant risk factor for heroin use. In fact, 80 percent of heroin users first misuse prescription opioids.

Amphetamines and Methamphetamine
Amphetamines and methamphetamine are highly addictive synthetic stimulants (also known as speed) that mimic cocaine

but with much longer-lasting effects. Taken orally, smoked, or injected, stimulants produce a burst of energy that can quickly turn to anxiety, depression, paranoia, and psychosis.

Hallucinogens

Hallucinogens may be synthetic or natural compounds and include lysergic acid diethylamide (LSD), psilocybin mushrooms, ecstasy, and phencyclidine (PCP). Taken orally, hallucinogens inhibit the release of serotonin and alter mood, thought, and perception. Sensory input becomes jumbled and distorted; the brain loses its ability to perceive reality; and anxiety, panic, and psychosis may result.

Nicotine

Nicotine, the addictive substance in tobacco, stimulates the release of dopamine and norepinephrine. Although it does not produce intoxication or mental impairment, it does elevate heart rate and blood pressure and pose severe health threats. Since this book was first published in 2003, smoking-related illnesses have continued to account for approximately one out of every five deaths per year in the United States—more than the total annual deaths from alcohol and illicit drugs combined.

Words of Wisdom

Loving an addict is almost certain to produce many anxious moments. Here are some meditations and slogans heard in Twelve Step programs, as well as words of wisdom from others who have been there.

Serenity Prayer
God, grant me the serenity
to accept the things I cannot change,
courage to change the things I can,
and wisdom to know the difference.

- Faith is the substance of things hoped for, the evidence of things not seen. (Hebrews 2:1)
- You didn't cause it, you can't control it, and you can't cure it.
- If nothing changes, nothing changes.
- Progress, not perfection.
- God's never in a hurry, but he's always on time.
- In God's time, not my time.
- One day at a time.
- In nature there are no rewards or punishments. There are consequences.
- First things first.
- Live and let live.

- Easy does it.
- How important is it?
- Keep it simple.
- There but for the grace of God go I.
- Let go and let God.
- This, too, shall pass.
- Recovery is a journey, not a destination.
- Keep an open mind.
- Decisions aren't forever.
- It takes time.
- Change is a process, not an event.
- Fear is the darkroom where negatives are developed.
- Before engaging your mouth, put your mind in gear.
- There is no chemical solution to a spiritual problem.
- Spirituality is the ability to get our minds off ourselves.
- The first step in overcoming mistakes is to admit them.
- Formula for failure: trying to please everyone.
- A journey of a thousand miles begins with a single step.
- Trying to pray is praying.
- We're responsible for the effort, not the outcome.
- Minds are like parachutes—they won't work unless they're open.
- It isn't the load that weighs us down; it's the way we carry it.
- Serenity is not freedom from the storm but peace amid the storm.
- The seven Ts: take time to think the thing through.
- The results are in God's hands.

- We are not human beings having spiritual experiences; we are spiritual beings having human experiences.
- It's a pity we can't forget our troubles the same way we forget our blessings.
- Active addicts don't have relationships; they take hostages.
- Every day is a gift; that is why we call it the present.
- Recovery works for people who believe in God; recovery works for people who don't believe in God. Recovery never works for people who believe they *are* God.
- Just for today, I will try to live through this day only and not tackle my whole life's problems at once. I can do something for twelve hours that would appall me if I felt that I had to keep it up for a lifetime.
- There are two days in every week over which we have no control: yesterday and tomorrow. Today is the only day we can change.
- Pain is the touchstone of spiritual growth.
- The road to disappointment is paved with expectations.
- Depression is anger turned inward.

Resources

Local chapters of Alcoholics Anonymous, Narcotics Anonymous, Al-Anon, and Nar-Anon can be found in most communities. They are all good sources of information and support. Additionally, private and public agencies that treat addiction usually offer educational materials and programs for families. For more information, contact any of the following organizations:

Al-Anon Family Group Headquarters, Inc.
1600 Corporate Landing Parkway
Virginia Beach, VA 23454-5617
(757) 563-1600; (888) 4AL-ANON (meeting information)
www.al-anon.org

Alcoholics Anonymous World Services, Inc.
General Service Office
P.O. Box 459
Grand Central Station
New York, NY 10163
(212) 870-3400
www.aa.org

Center for Substance Abuse Treatment (CSAT)
Substance Abuse and Mental Health Services Administration
    (SAMHSA)
5600 Fishers Lane
Rockville, MD 20857
(240) 276-1660; TTY: (800) 487-4889; (877) SAMHSA-7
www.samhsa.gov

Families Anonymous, Inc.
701 Lee Street, Suite 670
Des Plaines, IL 60016
(800) 736-9805
www.familiesanonymous.org

National Federation of Families
15800 Crabbs Branch Way
Suite 300
Rockville, MD 20855
(240) 403-1901
www.ffcmh.org

Hazelden Betty Ford Foundation
15251 Pleasant Valley Road
P.O. Box 11
Center City, MN 55012-2011
(800) 257-7810
www.hazeldenbettyford.org

Nar-Anon Family Groups
23110 Crenshaw Boulevard
Suite A
Torrance, CA 90505
(800) 477-6291; (310) 534-8188
www.nar-anon.org

Narcotics Anonymous World Services, Inc.
P.O. Box 9999
Van Nuys, CA 91409
(818) 773-9999
www.na.org

National Families in Action (NFIA)
P.O. Box 133136
Atlanta, GA 30333-3136
(404) 248-9676
www.nationalfamilies.org

SMART Recovery
7304 Mentor Avenue
Suite F
Mentor, OH 44060
(440) 951-5357
www.smartrecovery.org

Recommended Reading

For further reading on addiction and recovery, the following materials may be helpful:

Colleran, Carol, and Debra Jay. *Aging and Addiction: Helping Older Adults Overcome Alcohol or Medication Dependence.* Center City, MN: Hazelden Publishing, 2002.

Comunidades Latinas Unidas En Servicio (CLUES). *My Family, My Self: The Latino Guide to Emotional Well-Being.* Center City, MN: Hazelden Publishing, 2014.

Conyers, Beverly. *Everything Changes: Help for Families of Newly Recovering Addicts.* Center City, MN: Hazelden Publishing, 2009.

Conyers, Beverly. *The Recovering Heart: Emotional Sobriety for Women.* Center City, MN: Hazelden Publishing, 2013.

DuPont, Robert L. *The Selfish Brain: Learning from Addiction.* Center City, MN: Hazelden Publishing, 2000.

Hardiman, Michael. *Overcoming Addiction: A Common Sense Approach.* Freedom, CA: Crossing Press, 2000.

Jay, Debra. *It Takes a Family: Creating Lasting Sobriety, Togetherness, and Happiness,* 2nd ed. Center City, MN: Hazelden Publishing, 2021.

Jay, Jeff, and Debra Jay. *Love First: A Family's Guide to Intervention,* 3rd ed. Center City, MN: Hazelden Publishing, 2021.

Jay, Jeff, and Jerry Boriskin. *At Wit's End: What You Need to Know When a Loved One Is Diagnosed with Addiction and a Mental Illness.* Center City, MN: Hazelden Publishing, 2007.

Knapp, Carolyn. *Drinking: A Love Story.* New York: Dial Press, 1996, 2005.

McGovern, George. *Terry: My Daughter's Life-and-Death Struggle with Alcoholism.* New York: Villard Books, 1996.

Moyers, William Cope. *Now What? An Insider's Guide to Addiction and Recovery.* Center City, MN: Hazelden Publishing, 2012.

Nakken, Craig. *Reclaim Your Family from Addiction: How Couples and Families Recover Love and Meaning.* Center City, MN: Hazelden Publishing, 2000.

Peck, M. Scott. *The Road Less Traveled: A New Psychology of Love, Traditional Values, and Spiritual Growth (25th Anniversary Edition).* New York: Touchstone, 2012.

Prochaska, James O., John C. Norcross, and Carlo C. DiClemente. *Changing for Good.* New York: William Morrow, 1994.

Recovery Now: A Basic Text for Today. Center City, MN: Hazelden Publishing, 2013.

Salzberg, Sharon. *Lovingkindness: The Revolutionary Art of Happiness (25th Anniversary Edition).* Boston: Shambhala, 2020.

Sheff, David. *Beautiful Boy: A Father's Journey through His Son's Addiction.* Boston: Houghton Mifflin Company, 2009.

Sheff, David. *Clean: Overcoming Addiction and Ending America's Greatest Tragedy.* New York: Eamon/Dolan Mariner Books, 2014.

Notes

The number that begins each note indicates the page in this book where the cited material appears.

Introduction

4 **It's a depressing business:** Substance Abuse and Mental Health Services Administration (SAMHSA), *Key Substance Use and Mental Health Indicators in the United States: Results from the 2018 National Survey on Drug Use and Health* (August 2019), 2, https://store.samhsa.gov/sites/default/files/d7/priv/pep19-5068.pdf.

Chapter 1

9 **Drug overdose deaths in the United States have more than tripled:** Goodnough, Abby, "Overdose Deaths Have Surged During the Pandemic, C.D.C. Data Shows" *New York Times,* April 14, 2021, https://www.nytimes.com/2021/04/14/health/overdose-deaths-fentanyl-opiods-coronaviurs-pandemic.html. National Center for Health Statistics/NCHS Rapid Release Provisional Overdoes Death Counts," https://www.cdc.gov/nchs/nvss/vsrr/drug-overdose-data.htm.

10 **What's more, nonfatal drug-related poisonings:** Centers for Disease Control and Prevention (CDC) National Center for Injury Prevention and Control, *Annual Surveillance Report of Drug-Related Risks and Outcomes* (2019), 27, https://www.cdc.gov/drugoverdose/pdf/pubs/2019-cdc-drug-surveillance-report.pdf.

10 **And intentional overdose was the third leading method:** CDC NCHS, "Suicide and Self-Harm Injury," FastStats, last reviewed March 1, 2021, https://www.cdc.gov/nchs/fastats/suicide.htm.

10 **"The number of death certificates mentioning alcohol":** National Institute on Alcohol Abuse and Alcoholism,

"Alcohol-Related Deaths Increasing in the United States,"
news release, January 10, 2020, https://www.nih.gov/news
-events/news-releases/alcohol-related-deaths-increasing
-united-states.

10 **Beyond the statistics, addiction to alcohol or other
drugs can tear:** National Institute on Drug Abuse (NIDA),
"Criminal Justice DrugFacts," June 2020, https://www
.drugabuse.gov/publications/drugfacts/criminal-justice.

Chapter 3

43 **"Brain imaging studies of drug-addicted individuals":**
NIDA, "Drugs and the Brain," July 2020, https://www
.drugabuse.gov/publications/drugs-brains-behavior
-science-addiction/drugs-brain.

46 **"Addiction is a perversion of brain biology":** Robert L.
DuPont, *The Selfish Brain: Learning from Addiction*
(Center City, MN: Hazelden Publishing, 2000), 230.

Chapter 4

53 **While no specific "addiction gene":** Shatterproof, "The
Science of Addiction," https://www.shatterproof.org/about
-addiction/science-of-addiction.

56 **"[T]eens may crave the alleviation of negative emotions":**
FCD Prevention Works, "Effects of Drugs on the Teen
Brain," Hazelden Betty Ford Foundation, December 28,
2016, https://www.hazeldenbettyford.org/articles/fcd
/effects-drugs-teen-brain.

56 **Approximately 9.2 million adults:** SAMHSA, *Key Substance
Use and Mental Health Indicators,* 3, https://store.samhsa
.gov/sites/default/files/d7/priv/pep19-5068.pdf.

57 **"Most alcoholics I know experience that hunger":**
Carolyn Knapp, *Drinking: A Love Story* (New York: Dial
Press, 1996, 2005), 60.

57 **"More than 60 percent of people with bipolar disorder":** Bert Pepper, personal interview with the author, August 2002.

58 **Dr. DuPont adds a set of traits he defines as "character disorder":** DuPont, *The Selfish Brain,* 224.

Chapter 6

91 **The best-known model of change:** James O. Prochaska, John C. Norcross, and Carlo C. DiClemente, *Changing for Good* (New York: William Morrow & Co., 1994).

Chapter 7

126 **Professional treatment programs offer:** NIDA, "Treatment Approaches for Drug Addiction," January 2019, https://www.drugabuse.gov/publications/drugfacts /treatment-approaches-drug-addiction.

Chapter 9

155 **"Mindfulness is the simple and very powerful practice":** The Mindfulness Project, *I Am Here Now*, New York: TarcherPerigee, 2016.

Appendix A

164 **There is no precise measure:** DuPont. *The Selfish Brain*, 289.

172 **Heroin: "Synthetic opioids, including fentanyl":** NIDA, Fentanyl DrugFacts, https://www.drugabuse.gov/publications /drugfacts/fentanyl#ref.

173 **Prescription drugs: The federal government has taken steps:** Pradip K. Muhuri, Joseph C. Gfroerer, and M. Christine Davies, "Associations of Nonmedical Pain Reliever Use and Initiation of Heroin Use in the United States," *CBHSQ Data Review,* August 2013. NIDA, "Research on the Use and Misuse of Fentanyl and Other Synthetic Opioids," presentation to the House Committee on Energy and Commerce, Subcommittee on Oversight and Investigations, June 30, 2017.

174   **Nicotine: Since this book was first published:** American
      Medical Women's Association, *The Women's Complete
      Wellness Book,* edited by Debra R. Judelson and Diana L.
      Dell, New York: St. Martin's Press, 1998. CDC, Smoking and
      Tobacco Use, "Current Cigarette Smoking Among Adults
      in the United States," https://www.cdc.gov/tobacco/data
      _statistics/fact_sheets/adult_data/cig_smoking/ and
      "Health Effects of Cigarette Smoking," https://www.cdc.gov
      /tobacco/data_statistics/fact_sheets/health_effects/effects
      _cig_smoking/.

Acknowledgments

Dozens of people have very generously shared their intimate stories about addiction and recovery with me. Without their honesty and courage, I could not have written this book. In addition, many professionals in the treatment community contributed their knowledge and insight, including Valerie Fulginiti, LMHC; Debbie Galinski, LRC; Barbara K. George, LMHC; Dayna Gladstein, LICSW, CDP; Joseph Hyde, LMHC, CAS; and Bert Pepper, MD. To all, thank you.

About the Author

Beverly Conyers, MA, is a writer and college English teacher who lives in New England. A respected voice in recovery and wellness, she is also the author of *Everything Changes, The Recovering Heart, Find Your Light,* and *Follow Your Light.*

About Hazelden Publishing

As part of the Hazelden Betty Ford Foundation, Hazelden Publishing offers both cutting-edge educational resources and inspirational books. Our print and digital works help guide individuals in treatment and recovery, and their loved ones. Professionals who work to prevent and treat addiction also turn to Hazelden Publishing for evidence-based curricula, digital content solutions, and videos for use in schools, treatment and correctional programs, and community settings. We also offer training for implementation of our curricula.

Through published and digital works, Hazelden Publishing extends the reach of healing and hope to individuals, families, and communities affected by addiction and related issues.

For more information about Hazelden publications,
please call **800-328-9000**
or visit us online at **hazelden.org/bookstore**.

Other Titles by Beverly Conyers

Everything Changes
Help for Families of Newly Recovering Addicts
Everything Changes assuages fears and uncertainty by teaching loved ones of newly recovering addicts how to navigate the often-tumultuous early months of recovery. Beverly Conyers, author of the acclaimed *Addict in the Family,* again shares the hope and knowledge that she gained as a parent of a recovering addict by focusing on the aftermath of addiction.
Order No. 3807, also available as an ebook

The Recovering Heart
Emotional Sobriety for Women
Beverly Conyers, a prominent voice in recovery, uses personal stories and informed insight to guide you in achieving emotional sobriety by addressing behaviors and feelings unique to the female experience.
Order No. 3969, also available as an ebook

Find Your Light
Practicing Mindfulness to Recover from Anything
Author Beverly Conyers has guided hundreds of thousands of readers through the process of recognizing family roles in addiction, healing shame, building healthy relationships, releasing trauma, focusing on emotional sobriety, as well as acknowledging self-sabotaging behaviors, addictive tendencies, and substance use patterns. With her newest work, she shows us how the practice of mindfulness can be a game-changing part of recovering from anything and everything.
Order No. 3591, also available as an ebook

Other Titles That May Interest You

Living Without Shame
A Support Book for Mothers with Addicted Children
Barbara Theodosiou

Living Without Shame is the follow-up support book to Barbara Theodosiou's family account of addiction, *Without Shame*. She knows all too well the depths of addiction, losing her precious son Daniel to its destruction. Recipient of a White House Champion of Change award, Barbara Theodosiou continues to help other mothers of addicted children with this interactive mindfulness journal for moms.

Order No. 3562

Love First
A Family's Guide to Intervention
Jeff Jay and Debra Jay

This revised and expanded third edition of the gold standard for intervention provides clear steps for harnessing the power of family, friends, and professionals to create a better future with loved ones who have an addiction.

Order No. 8853, also available as an ebook

It Takes a Family
Creating Lasting Sobriety, Togetherness, and Happiness
Debra Jay

This second edition of the groundbreaking book by acclaimed interventionist and educator Debra Jay celebrates the unique and powerful role families play in successful long-term recovery from addiction. Readers receive tips, tools, and a framework for pursuing the proven path of Structured Family Recovery.®

Order No. 8854, also available as an ebook

Hazelden books are available at fine bookstores everywhere.
To order directly from Hazelden, call **800-328-9000**
or visit **hazelden.org/bookstore**.